ony

The Language of MAPS

Fearon Teacher Aids, a division of

David S. Lake Publishers

Belmont, California

MAKEMASTER® Blackline Masters

Photo 3 reprinted, by permission, from "Remote Sensing: Connecticut River Valley," *Journal of Geography,* January 1980, p. 39. NASA photograph.

Photo 4 reprinted, by permission, by P G & E Company. NASA photograph.

Maps 3, 4, and 5 reprinted, by permission, from *The California Geographer,* vol. 14, (1973—74), pp. 30—31.

Map 11 and sections of Group Activities D, E, and F adapted, by permission, from *The Pennsylvania Geographer,* vol. 7 (1), February 1969, pp. 1—6.

Editor: Gustavo Medina
Cover and text designer: Terry McGrath
Illustrators: Duane Bibby and Terry McGrath
Production editor: Robert E. Wanetick
Design manager: Susan True
Manufacturing manager: Susan Siegel

ISBN—0—8224—4242—6

Printed in the United States of America

1.9 8 7 6 5 4 3

Contents

PART II Self-Directed Activities 55

Preface

Today there is a summons to return to basics. Many educators contend that getting along with one's fellow beings is the most basic skill of all. Each of us, regardless of our own point of view, would agree heartily on the importance of this concept. However, the public's summons—for better or for worse—is for the basic skills of reading, writing, and arithmetic.

This book is a unique attempt to meet both demands in a practical, real-life way through the use of the language of maps. Through teacher-directed and self-directed student activities centering on map concepts, students are encouraged to use and develop "the three Rs."

Part I contains 25 structured, teacher-directed lessons with titles, objectives, preparation suggestions, lesson procedures, and follow-up activities. Part II contains 25 self-directed student activities and map exercises.

As you use these lessons and activities, you will find that your students—regardless of age—will develop confidence in themselves, learn about their environment, and improve their basic skills. They will be reading words that will help them become more aware of their relationship to this planet and their environment, and they ultimately will be reading the printed symbolism of maps. Most important, your students will be able to apply immediately what they learn.

I have used lessons like these with groups of varying sizes, ages, and educational backgrounds, from prekindergarten children to teachers and graduate students. Although the language and format of this book is geared to the middle grades, the lessons and activities are easy to adapt for any age group. I invite comments from any users of this book about any problems, successes, or new ideas for implementing the map concepts and skills.

Haig A. Rushdoony

Introduction

This book is divided substantively into two parts: Part I, Teacher-Directed Lessons, and Part II, Self-Directed Activities. Part III is the answer key, and Part IV consists of numbered photos and maps to be used with Parts I and II. Parts I and II contain parallel sections—Orientation and Direction, Symbolization, Location and Distance, and Inferential Reading—to be used together.

Use of Part I

Part I is the foundation for teaching and learning map skills. It contains precise lesson plans developed sequentially within each section *and* from section to section. Each lesson comprises the following components:

> Lesson title
> Objective
> Preparation
> Lesson
> Follow-up

The *lesson title* focuses your attention on the primary *objective*. Most objectives are precise. However, the level of competency is left to your discretion in some lessons.

The *preparation* spells out the materials you will need and, at times, the special setting or circumstances for the learning experience. Although each preparation section is precise, you have the option of preparing or duplicating materials in any way that best suits you and your students' needs.

The *lesson* provides developmentally prepared procedures and alternatives.

The *follow-up* indicates at least one additional activity or experience you may use with the entire class or for a selected few to reinforce the objective of the lesson.

Use of Parts II, III, and IV

Part II is designed for self-directed student activities. These 25 activities may be duplicated and placed in a student learning center for individual use or for class use as follow-ups to the teacher-directed lessons where appropriate. After completing a section of the teacher-directed lessons, students should easily be able to work any of the activities in the corresponding self-directed section.

Part III, the answer key, goes hand in hand with Part II. All activities in Part II are self-directive and, with the key, self-corrective.

Part IV contains the visuals that accompany the self-directed activities in Part II. In some cases it may be advisable to use a projector rather than to duplicate a visual.

If any of your students have difficulty doing the activities, you may wish to consider any of the following options: (1) read the activity aloud and work through it cooperatively in a small group; (2) place students in pairs to complete the activity together; or (3) record the activities on tapes or cassettes and allow the students to work through them with the accompanying visuals.

PART I

Teacher-Directed Lessons

Orientation and Direction

Lesson 1 Finding Directions at Noon

OBJECTIVE

to identify the four main, or cardinal, directions outdoors at noon

PREPARATION

Note: If you are living in the Southern Hemisphere, the directions at noon (Chart 1) will be reversed. With your back to the sun, you are facing south, east is to your left, and so forth.

MATERIALS
Chart 1, copied on 20-by-24-inch oaktag (see page 7)

NEW TERMS
cardinal directions
main directions

TIME
a sunny day shortly before or after noon

PLACE
classroom and schoolyard

LESSON

1. Show Chart 1 and have the class read the directions aloud. **Say:** *These four directions —north, east, south, and west —are called **main** or **cardinal directions.** Let us see how well we can tell the main or cardinal directions today using the sun at noon.*

2. Take the class outside and have students choose places to stand with the sun at their backs.

3. Hold up Chart 1 for everyone to see.

4. Ask students to point to north, east, south, and west.

5. Have students move to different positions in the schoolyard and reorient themselves. Again have them point out directions. Vary the use of the chart by **asking** *What direction is to your right?* and similiar questions.

6. Have each student face the direction he or she would go to return home from school. Have each student name which direction it is. If students face noncardinal directions, explain that those are in-between, or intermediate, directions and that they will be discussed in a later lesson.

FOLLOW-UP

➤Using Chart 1 in the morning or the late afternoon, have students determine directions by reading and interpreting the Directions at Noon chart. **Say:** *When the sun was behind you at noon, what did you notice in front of you?* (for example, the flagpole or the greenhouse across the street) *When the sun was at your back, what direction were you facing?* (north) *The flagpole (or the greenhouse) is in what direction from here?* (north) Explain to the students that they have begun to use landmarks and that landmarks can be important in finding their way.

Lesson 1 (continued)	
	➤ To make students aware of seasonal changes, between the twentieth and twenty-third days of several successive months trace the children's shadows at noon on pieces of butcher paper. Cut out the shadows and have the students write their names, the date, and the time on them. Each month, compare each student's shadow dolls to determine the lengthening or shortening of the shadow. (The higher the sun in the sky, the shorter the shadow; the lower the sun, the longer the shadow. Winter shadows will be longer and summer shadows shorter. The shadows will be the same length in September and March, the autumnal and vernal equinoxes.) ➤ Have students measure the lengths of shadows either weekly to note changes over time or at different times during the day to discover that shadows are shortest around noontime.

Lesson 2   *Using a Compass*

OBJECTIVE

to identify the four main or cardinal directions indoors and outdoors with the use of a compass

PREPARATION

MATERIALS

Chart 2, copied on 24-by-36-inch oaktag (see page 7)

Chart 3, copied on 24-by-36-inch oaktag (see page 7) or a chart patterned after the compass you use

magnetic compass

map or globe showing the North and South Magnetic Poles

chalk

TIME

social studies, science, or mathematics class

PLACE

classroom and schoolyard

LESSON

1. Hold up Chart 2 and review how the class determined the four directions outside.

2. **Ask:** *How can we tell directions indoors?* Encourage the students to look outside to find familiar landmarks that they spotted when determining directions with the noon sun.

3. **Ask:** *If it were not sunny or we did not look or go outside, what would be another way to tell directions?*

4. Display Chart 3 and explain the use of the compass. **Say:** *The compass has a needle and directions on it. The needle is a magnet that points to the nearest magnetic pole.* Show the North and South Poles on a map or globe. **Ask:** *Which pole will our compass needle point to?* Tell the students that the needle can be attracted by iron—their belt buckles, watches, and desks may pull the compass needle off course. Explain to students that the magnetic poles are magnetic fields, not set points, and can vary in location.

5. Place Chart 2 on the floor and put the compass on top of it, shifting the chart to match the north and south markings on the compass with those on the chart.

6. Take the class out to the schoolyard and repeat step 5. Mark directions with chalk on a sidewalk or a paved surface.

FOLLOW-UP

➤ Make north, east, south, and west directional cards and have students pin cards on the appropriate walls of the classroom.

➤ Play a game in which you **say:** *I'm thinking of something that is ＿＿＿* (for example, a color), or *I see something that looks like a ＿＿＿. Which direction is it from where you are sitting?* Students determine what the object is by asking questions, then identify its location (for example, north wall or east part of the room).

DIRECTIONS AT NOON

Stand with your back to the sun.
You are facing north.
East is to your right.
West is to your left.
South is in back of you.

CHART 1

MAIN DIRECTIONS

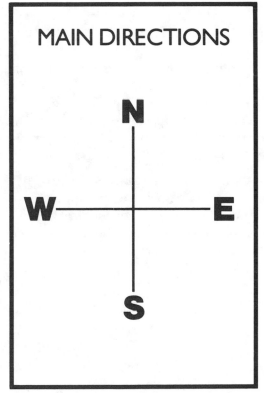

CHART 2

A COMPASS

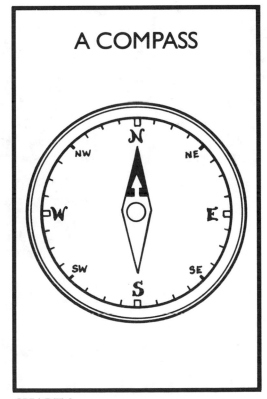

CHART 3

Lesson 3

Telling Directions in Three Ways

OBJECTIVE

to recall and explain at least two ways in which directions were determined in lessons 1 and 2

PREPARATION

MATERIALS
Charts 1, 2, and 3 (see page 7)
magnetic compass

TIME
social studies class

PLACE
classroom and schoolyard

LESSON

1. Remind students that they have learned three ways to tell directions. **Ask:** *What are the ways to tell directions?* If necessary, give clues by **saying** *How did we find directions using the noon sun?* (Charts 1 and 2) *What if it were not a sunny day?* (a place, a landmark, or a compass) *How did we find directions by using a compass?* (needle or arrow pointed north)

2. Clarify any point of the above as needed, including the fact that the use of the noon sun to find directions is determined by the earth – sun relationship, that the movement of the compass needle is determined by the magnetic poles, and so forth.

FOLLOW-UP

➤ Use a flashlight or a bright lamp that you can hold comfortably and that allows you plenty of mobility. Choose four students to hold up directional cards—north, south, east, and west. Have students stand at the appropriate places in the classroom that represent the four directions. **Say:** *I will be the sun and I will be walking in a circle behind you, the four directions. When I stop behind one of you and shine the light, I want all of you to say out loud and in turn what direction you now are.*

➤ You can vary this activity by having students state the "new" directions in clockwise or counterclockwise order. You can have students trade places to match the new directions. Or divide the class into groups of four and have them compete by timing how long it takes each group to state the new directions or assume the new positions.

Lesson 4

Finding Intermediate Directions

OBJECTIVE

to identify in-between, or intermediate, directions

PREPARATION

MATERIALS
Chart 3 (see page 7)
Chart 4, copied on 20-by-24-inch oaktag (see page 10)
Chart 5, copied on 24-by-36-inch oaktag (see page 10)
magnetic compass
felt-tip pen or crayon

NEW TERMS
in-between directions
intermediate directions

TIME
social studies class

PLACE
classroom

LESSON

1. Show Chart 4 and have the class read the intermediate directions aloud. Use a compass with Chart 5 to show how northeast (NE) is between north and east. **Say:** *Northeast is called an **in-between** or **intermediate direction**. Let's see how many other in-between or intermediate directions we can find.*

2. Using Charts 3 and 4, **ask:** *Which direction is between south and west?* (southwest) Continue with similar questions until the class has identified each intermediate direction.

3. **Ask:** *Between which cardinal directions is northwest?* Continue questioning until students have identified all the intermediate directions.

4. Have volunteers place a compass on Chart 5 and match north on the compass with north on the chart.

5. Have students identify direction lines on Chart 5 by matching the lines with corresponding lines on the compass and writing *NE, SW, S,* and so forth.

6. Compare Chart 5 with Charts 3 and 4 and the compass for accuracy. Have the class point out all eight directions in the classroom.

7. Review by **asking** *Which directions are the main, or cardinal, directions? Which are the in-between, or intermediate, directions?*

FOLLOW-UP

➤Write the words *northeast, northwest, southeast,* and *southwest* on separate cards. Mix the cards with the directional cards from the follow-up in lesson 2. Have students pin the cards on the appropriate walls of the classroom.

➤Using all eight directions, play a game in which you **say:** *I'm thinking of something that is _____* (for example, a color) or *I see something that looks like a _____. Which direction is it from where you are sitting?* Students determine what the object is by asking questions, then identify its location (for example, northwest wall or southeast part of the room).

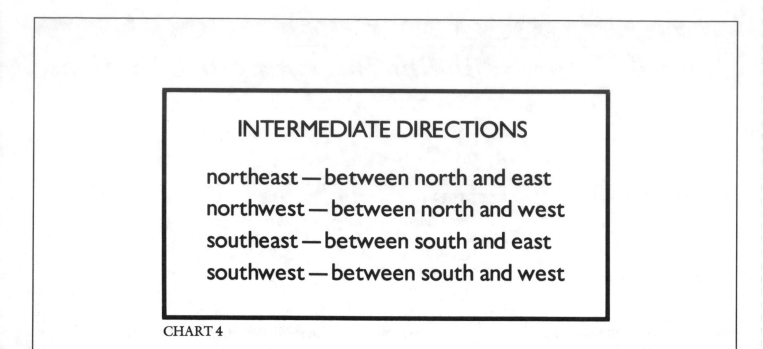

INTERMEDIATE DIRECTIONS

northeast — between north and east

northwest — between north and west

southeast — between south and east

southwest — between south and west

CHART 4

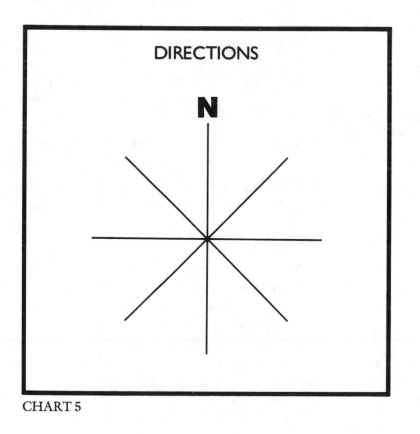

CHART 5

Lesson 5

Using a Compass to Find Directions

OBJECTIVE

to use a compass to identify and record the cardinal and intermediate directions when given either the north or south directional line

PREPARATION

MATERIALS

Group Activity A, one copy for each student (see page 12); mark half the papers with *N* at the top, as in Chart 5 (see page 10), and the other half with an *S* at the bottom
transparency of Group Activity A
clear transparency
overhead projector
transparency pen or crayon
compasses, one for each student or group of students
Charts 1– 5 (see pages 7 and 10)
directional cards from follow-ups in lessons 2 and 4

TIME

reading or social studies class

PLACE

classroom

LESSON

1. Distribute Group Activity A and the compasses. Have the students write their names on their papers. Project the transparency of Group Activity A.

2. Have each student place the compass in the center of the activity sheet and align the paper's north – south line with the compass needle.

3. Have the students mark the directions (N, NE, and so forth) on the activity sheet.

4. After all the students have marked the directions on the activity sheets, fill in the directions on the transparency.

5. Have the students check one another's papers against the projected transparency or with the chart and a compass on the floor.

FOLLOW-UP

➤ Play a game using a compass and directional cards. For example, have one student walk five steps northwest and two steps east. Have another student walk five steps northeast and two steps west from the same place. Ask each student which direction he or she is facing. (They should be face to face, one facing east and the other facing west.)

➤ Play a game using a compass. Have a student walk two steps north, two steps east, two steps south, and two steps west. Ask the class what happened. (The student ended up where he or she began.) Ask the class in what shape or area the student walked. (square) Try other patterns, for example, two steps south, four steps west, two steps north, and four steps east (rectangle).

Name _____

GROUP ACTIVITY A

Using a Compass to Find the Cardinal and Intermediate Directions

Complete the following sentence.

The compass needle or arrow points to north in our classroom, where on

the wall I see _____

_____

_____

_____

_____

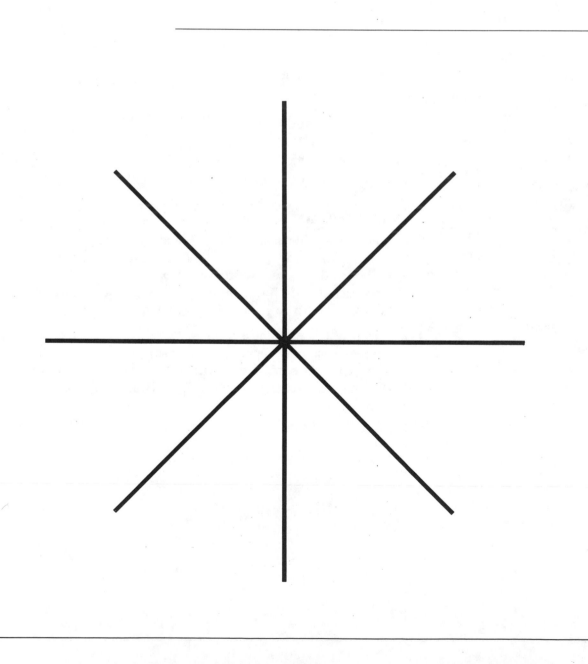

Lesson 6

Orienting Yourself on a Map

OBJECTIVE

to identify at least four ways to orient yourself on a map

PREPARATION

MATERIALS

Figures 1 and 2, copied on 24-by-36-inch oaktag (see pages 14 and 15)
four clear transparencies
overhead projector
transparency pen or crayon
Figure 1, copy for each student for follow-up

NEW TERMS

compass rose

TIME

social studies class

PLACE

classroom

LESSON

1. **Say:** *We have been orienting ourselves indoors and outside using a compass, the sun, or a landmark. Today we are going to see how we can orient ourselves on a map so we'll know which way to go to find something or someplace.*

2. Show Figure 1. **Say:** *This is called a **compass rose.** It shows us directions. How many of you have seen a compass rose before? Where? In an atlas? On a map?*

3. **Say:** *Directions on a map may be shown in different ways. Let's look at four ways.* Show Figure 2. **Ask:** *Which map uses a compass rose?* (A) *Which way is north on this map?* (top) *South?* (bottom) *East?* (right) *West?* (left)

4. **Ask:** *How can we tell directions on Map B?* (words) **Ask:** *How can we tell directions on Map C?* (arrow and letter *N*)

5. **Ask:** *Can you guess how we tell directions on Map D?* (lines) *How do we know which way is north?* (Converging lines are north-south lines, and parallel lines are east-west lines.) *What might help if we cannot tell whether north is at the top or the bottom?* (add North Pole and South Pole) *Which way is south on Map D?* (bottom) *East?* (right) *West?* (left) Explain that if there is no word or symbol indicating directions, north is always at the top of the map.

6. Sum up by **asking** *What are four ways that we could orient ourselves on these maps?* (compass rose; words; directional arrow with letter; lines on map or no directions means top is north)

FOLLOW-UP

➤ Remind students that the four main directions on the compass rose are called cardinal directions. Point out that the names of the intermediate directions on the compass rose of Figure 1 are not shown. Show the intermediate directions on the compass rose — northeast, southeast, southwest, and northwest. Distribute copies of Figure 1 and have the students fill in the intermediate directions on the compass rose.

FIGURE 1 *A Compass Rose*

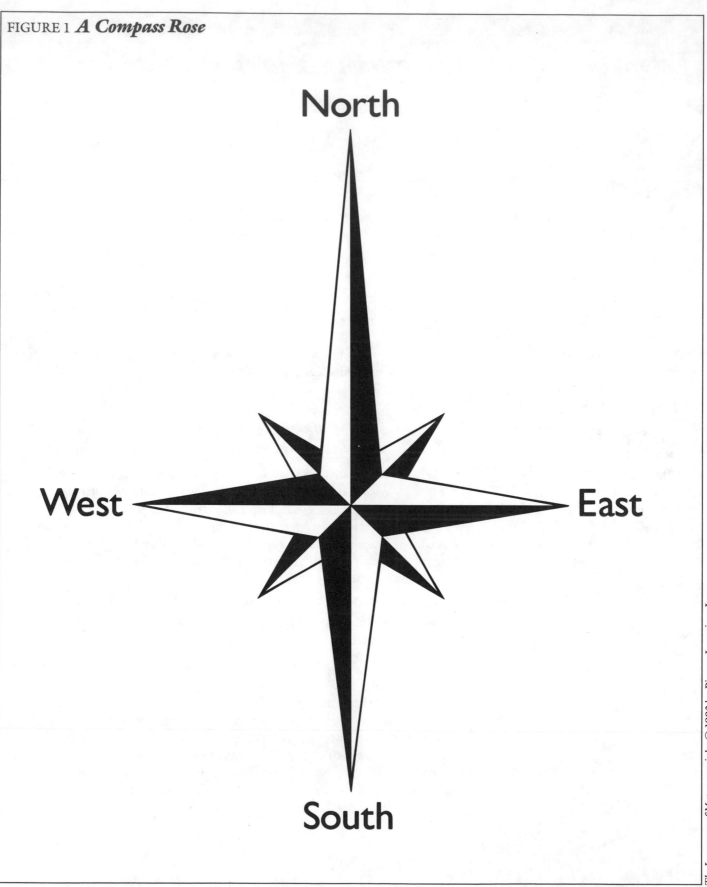

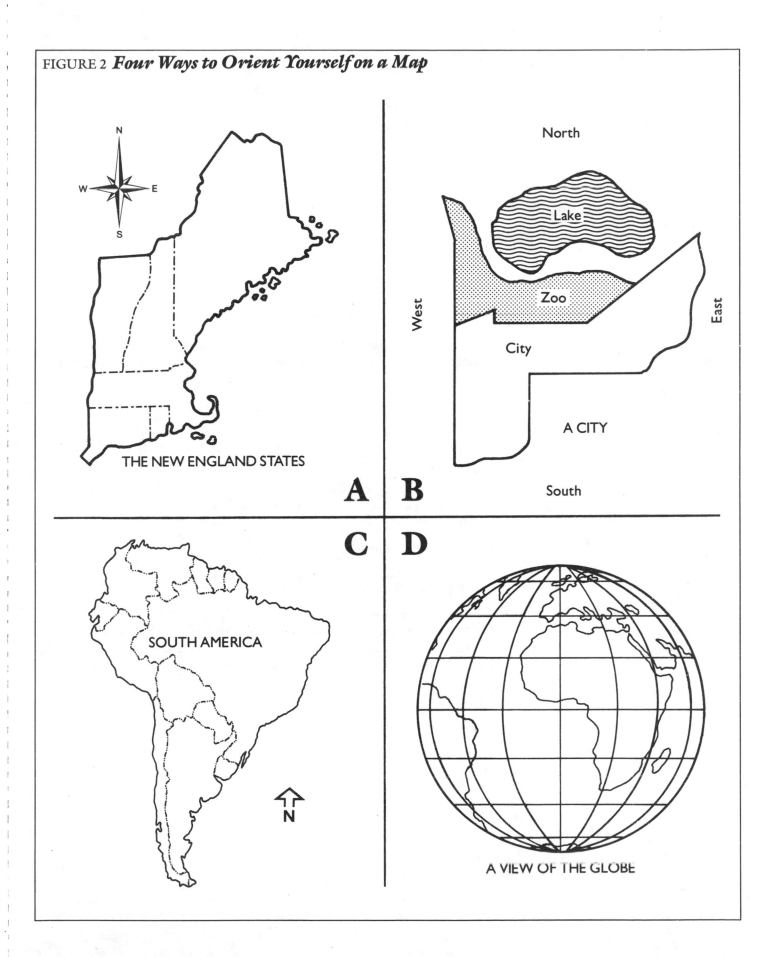

FIGURE 2 *Four Ways to Orient Yourself on a Map*

A THE NEW ENGLAND STATES

B A CITY

C SOUTH AMERICA

D A VIEW OF THE GLOBE

Symbolization

Lesson 7 — Viewing the Earth from an Elevated Area

OBJECTIVE

to observe and record at least three landmarks in the neighborhood or on the earth's surface from a hill or from an aerial photo

PREPARATION

Note: If you do not have access to an elevated area, cannot take a trip beyond the school grounds, or do not have a photo or slide of the school or community area, project Photo 1 and conduct this lesson in the classroom without referring to directions. Have students observe the photo and proceed directly to step 2. The following landmarks may easily be observed on Photo 1: lake, park along upper lake shore, houses, streets, walkways, trees, shrubs, and open space.

MATERIALS
Chart 1 (see page 7)
magnetic compasses
instant-developing camera
paper and pencil for each student
Photo 1 (see page 100) if field trip is
   not possible

TIME
scheduled field trip or social studies
   class

PLACE
elevated area or classroom

LESSON

1. Walk to the top of a nearby hill, elevated area, or tower where the neighborhood can be observed and students can orient themselves with the sun, with compasses, or with both.

2. Divide the class into groups. Each group is to make observations in a different direction. Have groups take directional bearings using compasses and have each group member note or sketch observed phenomena. Take a photograph of the phenomena indicated by each group.

3. Have groups rotate and continue their observations until each group has recorded observations in all four cardinal directions.

4. Return to the classroom and share observations, sketches, notes, and photos.

5. Have each group combine the members' observations into a list or a sketch of what they saw in each direction. Remind students to note what things the others observed but they missed.

6. Review and compare findings.

FOLLOW-UP

➤ Display sketches, lists, and photos in the classroom and have students prepare a label for each one (for example, Looking South from Smokey Hill), or make labels on cards and have students match labels with appropriate sketches, lists, or photos. Color-code the backs of matching sets so that students can check the accuracy of their matches. Place all sets in your learning area for students to use as a matching game.

Lesson 8 — *Being a Photo Detective*

OBJECTIVE

to identify at least three landmarks from a quick look at a photograph and to write an appropriate title for the photograph

PREPARATION

Note: Before students do this activity on their own, conduct a group practice activity, ideally with two projectors—one to project a photo (from social studies text or elsewhere) and one with a blank transparency for listing or sketching what students observe.

If you used Photo 1 in the previous lesson, students will have had some practice in being "photo detectives," and you may choose to forgo the practice activity.

MATERIALS
Photos 2A, 2B, and 3 (see pages 101 and 102) or aerial or terrestrial photos of your school area
two overhead projectors, or one overhead projector and one opaque projector
transparency pen or crayon
paper, two sheets for each student
social studies textbook

TIME
social studies class

LESSON

1. **Say:** *Today we're going to play a game called Photo Detectives. Here's what you'll do. When you see this photo* (project Photo 2A), *look at it carefully to remember as much as you can about what you see. You will have only 15 seconds to see the photo.*

   When I turn off the projector, you will have two minutes to list or sketch everything you saw in the photo. When I say Stop, finish any word, phrase, or part of a sketch you have already started and put your pencil down.

   After you have recorded what you saw in the photo, I will signal you to write a title that best fits the photo.

2. If giving points, **say:** *Here is how points will be scored:*
   Two points for every correct observation and title, regardless of spelling or how your sketch looks.
   Minus one point for anything you included that was not in the photo.

3. **Say:** *Let's play the game together. You will now see a photo for 15 seconds.* Project Photo 2B for 15 seconds. **Say:** *Now write or sketch what you observed in the photo. Don't be concerned about your spelling or art work. Just get your observations down on the paper. You have two minutes.*

4. After two minutes, **say:** *Stop.* Permit each student to finish sketching or writing. **Say:** *Put your pencils down.* When the class is ready, **say:** *What is a good title for this photo? Write it near the bottom of your paper.*

5. When the students have finished, project the photo again to check the recorded data. Move around the room and help students to total their points.

6. When the class is ready, project Photo 3 for 15 seconds. **Say:** *Now write or sketch what you observed in this photo. Don't be concerned about your spelling or art work. Just get your observations recorded on your paper. Remember, you have only two minutes.*

7. After two minutes, **say:** *Stop.* Then **say:** *Write the best title for this photo near the bottom of your paper.*

8. When the students have finished, project the photo again to check the recorded data. Move around the room and help students to total their points.

Lesson 8 (continued)

9. Repeat step 6 with Photo 3 as often as needed or for as long as students are interested. Vary the time as needed.

10. Repeat step 6 with other photos from your social studies textbook or elsewhere.

FOLLOW-UP

➤ Set up a learning center with a timer for children to play Photo Detectives on their own or in pairs. Provide copies of Photos 1, 2A, and 2B or other photos. Students should study the photos for a given amount of time, then turn them face down.

➤ Have students go outside in pairs or small groups, select a direction, observe the area for 15 seconds, turn away, and record their observations. Students also may do this observation activity by looking out the classroom window for a given time, then turning away to record what they saw.

Lesson 9

Comparing a Photo with a Map

OBJECTIVE

to match symbols on a map with real images on a photo and to add at least one symbol to the map by reading and interpreting the photo

PREPARATION

Note: By preparing transparencies of Photos 1 and 2A and Map 1, you can superimpose Map 1 onto the photos to verify which photo has been mapped.

MATERIALS
Photos 1 and 2, copies, transparencies, or opaque projections (see pages 100 and 101)
Map 1 (see page 104), copy or transparency, and one copy for each student
overhead or opaque projector
clear transparency
transparency pen or crayon

TIME
social studies or geography class

NEW TERMS
key
phenomena
symbol

LESSON

1. Distribute Map 1 to students. Show Photos 1 and 2A to determine which photo has been mapped. **Ask:** *Which photo do you have a map of?* (Map 1) *How can you tell?* Place Map 1 over each photo (if you use a transparency) so students can visualize the reasons, or match various shapes and phenomena on the photo with map symbols.

2. **Say:** *Phenomena are things (living and nonliving), places or landmarks, and people on earth. Some of these phenomena are shown on maps. What phenomena are shown on Map 1?* (See map for answers.) *How are they shown?* (symbols)

3. **Say:** *Symbols on a map may be shown with lines, dots, or points; with area or space; and with colors or shadings. We find the symbols for a map in the map's key.* Point to the key on the map. **Say:** *This is called a key. It is important because it tells us what the symbols on the map mean. The key "unlocks" the symbols on the map for us.*

4. **Ask:** *What are the symbols in the key of this map?* Go over each one, pointing it out on the map. **Ask:** *What else could we add to the map?* Record the answers. **Ask:** *How shall we show them? What symbols should we make?* Allow the students to suggest symbols.

5. Have the students add symbols they have decided on to the key on their maps while you do the same on the clear transparency over the map. Continue with two or three more symbols, depending on class interest and need. Stress that symbols may be whatever we determine them to be. **Say:** *Some map symbols give us clues or ideas as to what they stand for or represent; for example, a small airplane can represent an airport, a triangle can be a mountain, and a wiggly line can mean a meandering river.*

6. **Ask:** *What would be the best title for this map?* List the choices on the chalkboard and help the class determine the most appropriate title. Have students write in the title on their maps as you do so on the transparency.

Lesson 9 (continued)

7. **Ask:** *How is the map different from the photo?* Give clues to obtain responses such as the following:
   - A symbol on a map *represents* something, while a photo is a *picture* of it.
   - We can use lines, dots, spaces, shadings, colorings as symbols. A symbol may represent anything we want it to be; it does not have to look like the real thing.
   - A photo includes everything the photographer and camera lens can take in, while a map includes only what the map maker puts in it. Therefore, a map may not show everything that the photo shows.

FOLLOW-UP

➤ Find other photos from which students can make maps using at least three symbols.

➤ Have the class locate maps in classroom and library books. Have the students draw symbols found in keys and explain what each symbol means.

➤ Encourage interested students to map their home or school areas or their favorite vacation spots using at least three symbols in each map.

Lesson 10   *Using Symbols to Show Elevation*

OBJECTIVE

to determine symbolically the four types of geographic landforms using a physical or physical-political map and a cross-section diagram

PREPARATION

Note: Project Figures 3, 4, and 5 or sketch them on the chalkboard. Use colored chalk to show elevation in Figure 5. (Use a map from your social studies textbook as a pattern.)

   MATERIALS
Figures 3, 4, and 5, sketched on chalkboard (see page 23)
Chart 6, copied on 24-by-36-inch oaktag (see page 23)
Map 2, copy for each student (see page 105)
overhead projector
transparency pen or crayon
social studies textbooks
photos or diagrams in social studies textbook illustrating the four basic geographic landforms—mountains, plateaus, hills, and lowlands or plains. (If you cannot find examples of the different ways of depicting elevation in textbooks, then proceed solely with Chart 6 and the figures on the chalkboard.)

   TIME
social studies or geography class

   NEW TERMS
contour lines
cross section
diagram
landforms
national boundary
physical map
physical-political map
plateau
political map

LESSON

1. **Say:** *A **diagram** is a sketch or plan that explains something by showing its parts. In maps, a diagram could be an aerial view of a mountain as shown by **contour lines.*** Show Figure 3. *Contour lines show elevation on a map by connecting all points that are the same height with one line. A side view, or **cross section,** also can be used.* Show Figure 4. *A cross section is a sketch or plan that shows something as though we had cut through it. For example, Figure 4 is a cross section of a mountain as we would see it from the side.*

2. Have the class turn to a page in their social studies text that contains a photo, diagram, or cross section of a landform (elevation). Point out that until now, everything has been symbolically represented as a flat surface. Help the students find other examples of elevation. Have the class note different ways elevation is shown: color, contour lines (Figure 3), shadings and lines (Figure 5), symbols, and cross section (Figure 4).

3. Show Map 2. Have the class turn to a page in the social studies text that shows a map similar to Map 2. **Ask:** *What is the title of this map?* (Landforms of South America) **Say:** *Four kinds of **landforms** are shown in the map key. What are the four kinds of landforms?* (mountains, plateaus, hills, plains or lowlands) Have the class show where each type of landform may be found on Map 2 and in the textbook map. Point out each type on Map 2. **Say:** *The landform symbols show us the physical features of South America. What does that mean?* (mountains, lowlands, etc., or how high or low the land is) *We call this kind of map a **physical map**.*

4. **Say:** *Besides the map symbols for the landforms and the Amazon River, there is one more symbol in the key. What is it?* (**national boundary** lines) **Ask:** *What do national boundary lines mean or do?* (They indicate the borders between nations.) **Say:** *Name a country shown on the map.* Accept several answers.

5. **Say:** *A map that shows countries with their national, or political, boundaries is called a **political map**. Map 2 is two kinds of maps in one, isn't it? What kind of a map is it?* (**physical-political map**) *Why?* [Symbols indicate physical features (elevation) and political separations (boundary lines) of countries.] *How do we know that it shows elevation?* (shadings, dots, lines, area or space on the key)

Lesson 10 (continued)

6. **Ask:** *What part of South America has the highest elevation?* (the west, or Pacific, coast and the northwest near the Caribbean Sea) *How high are the mountains along the Pacific coast?* (We're not given this information in this map.) *Are we shown where the lowest spot in South America is?* (no) *Which country seems to be all plains or lowlands?* (Uruguay) *What nation seems to have no plains or lowlands?* (Chile)

7. Show Chart 6 and **say:** *This chart shows a cross section of the elevation of South America. Remember, we looked at our school area from a high place. We looked at some aerial photos in which we were looking down at the earth. This chart shows us the earth as if we could cut into it and see a part of it. That is what a cross section does. The line marked A shows where sea level is.* **Ask:** *How does this help us picture the high and low spots of South America?* Help the students realize the answer if they have difficulty.

8. Referring to Chart 6, **ask:** *Which letter indicates the highest elevation?* (B) *Do you remember what range of mountains this is?* (Andes) You may want the class to follow the mountain chain northward on another map, identifying each range as you travel north. *Which letter shows the lowest part, or the plains?* (D) *Where do we see hills?* (C) *Where do we see other mountains in this cross section of South America?* (F) *What kind of landform does* E *represent? You may look at the map key, too.* (plateau) *Notice that a* **plateau** *is high and level. It is like a mountain without a peak.*

9. Review terms and elevation concepts on the chart and the map and in the textbook as needed to help students understand that lines, dots or points, and shadings on a map are symbolic means of depicting elevation, as are cross-section diagrams.

FOLLOW-UP

➤ Have clay available for students to work individually or in pairs using Figure 3 as a guide to make clay mountains.

➤ Have clay available for pairs of students to make clay cross sections of South America, using Chart 6 as a guide.

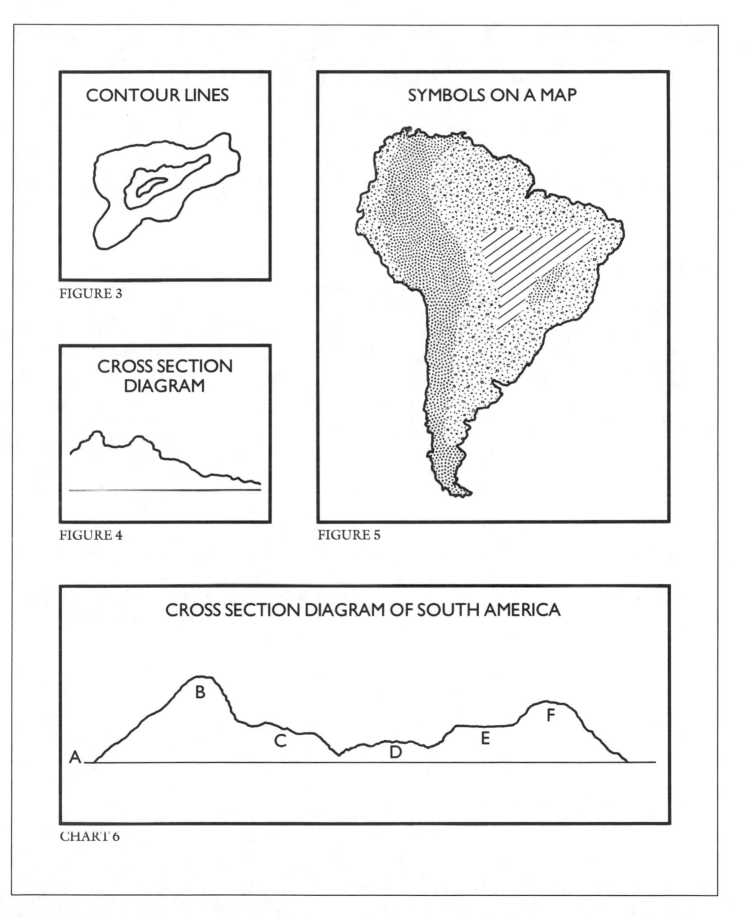

CONTOUR LINES

FIGURE 3

CROSS SECTION
DIAGRAM

FIGURE 4

SYMBOLS ON A MAP

FIGURE 5

CROSS SECTION DIAGRAM OF SOUTH AMERICA

A B C D E F

CHART 6

Lesson 11

Symbolizing Elevation in Different Ways

OBJECTIVE

to match two types of elevation diagrams with word descriptions

PREPARATION

MATERIALS
Group Activity B (see page 25), copied on 20-by-24-inch oaktag or projected on chalkboard, and copy for each student
overhead or opaque projector
chalk, transparency pen, or crayon

TIME
social studies class

LESSON

1. Distribute copies of Group Activity B to the students and have the students write their names on their papers.

2. Read the title and the word descriptions in part 1 aloud as a group. Explain that the task is to find which elevation (1–5) best fits each word description (A–E).

3. As a group, match each elevation and description, then read the correct answers and have students check their own work. (answers: A, 5; B, 1; C, 2; D, 4; E, 3)

4. Read the title and the descriptions in part 2 aloud as a group. **Say:** *This is a cross section showing different types of land. Let's match the word descriptions with the numbers on the cross section.* As a group, match elevations with word descriptions, then read the correct answers and have students check their own work. (answers: A, 3; B, 1; C, 5; D, 4; E, 2)

FOLLOW-UP

➤ Have students reconstruct each elevation in Activity B, part 1 with clay, matching the letters and numerals with the clay models.

➤ Have students work in groups of two or three to reconstruct the cross section in Activity B, part 2 with wet sand in an aquamarine or clear plastic shoe box. Have the students describe each landform aloud to the class or label each landform in the box.

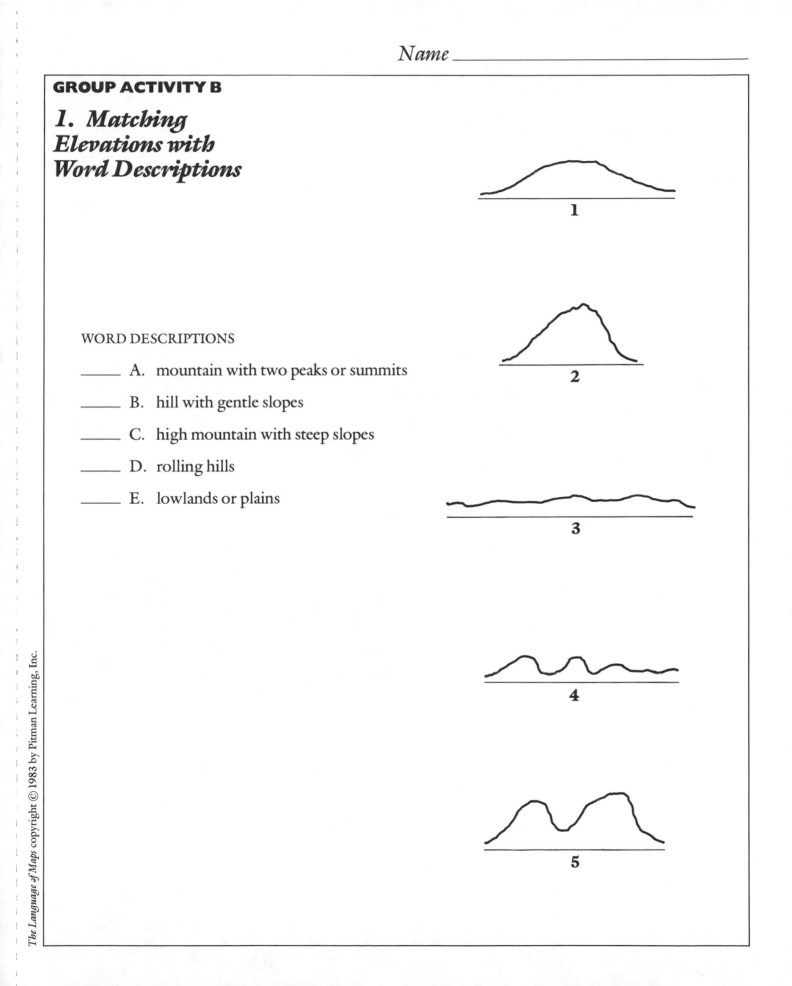

Name _____

GROUP ACTIVITY B

1. Matching Elevations with Word Descriptions

WORD DESCRIPTIONS

_____ A. mountain with two peaks or summits

_____ B. hill with gentle slopes

_____ C. high mountain with steep slopes

_____ D. rolling hills

_____ E. lowlands or plains

Name _____

2. *Matching Types of Landforms with Word Descriptions*

WORD DESCRIPTIONS

_____ A. lowlands or plains

_____ B. high mountain with steep west and east sides

_____ C. high mountain with steep east side

_____ D. plateau with sharp west side

_____ E. rolling hills or foothills

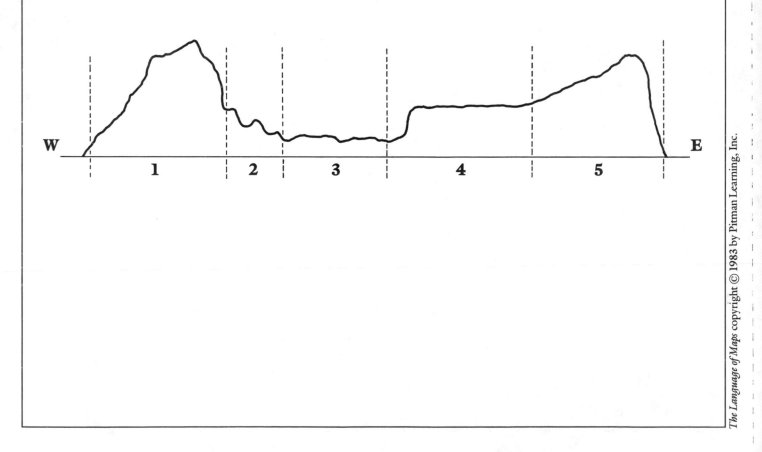

Lesson 12 *Using Contour Lines*

OBJECTIVE

to match elevations using cross-sectional and contour line symbols

PREPARATION

MATERIALS

Figure 6, copied on 20-by-24-inch oaktag or projected on chalkboard (see below)

Group Activity C (see page 28), transparency, or copied on 24-by-36-inch oaktag with clear transparency over it, and copy for each student if students are to do the activity individually

Photo 2B for Follow-Up

overhead or opaque projector

chalk, transparency pen, or crayon

TIME

social studies class

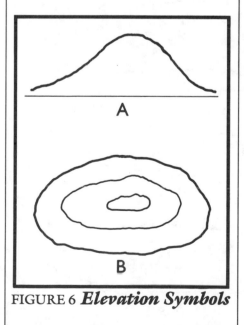

FIGURE 6 *Elevation Symbols*

LESSON

1. Explain Figure 6 to students by **saying** *A is a cross section of a mountain. B is an aerial view with* contour lines. Write both terms on chalkboard or on transparency under each symbol. **Say:** *You may remember from lesson 10 that contour lines give us an idea of the shape of the mountain as if we were looking down on it from above.*

2. **Say:** *Let's compare some other elevations.* Project Group Activity C. *In the left-hand column we have five cross sections of elevations.* (A– E) *On the right side, elevations are shown by contour lines.* (1– 5) *Let's match the lettered cross sections with the numbered contour lines.* **Ask:** *Where do you see the symbol for cross section A?* (2) Explain or have student explain why 2 is correct. Connect A and 2 and continue by **asking:** *What contour lines best match cross section B?* (1) Draw a line connecting B and 1. Continue with cross sections C (4), D (3), and E (5).

3. Repeat the exercise reversing the phrasing of the questions. For example, **ask:** *Which cross section or elevation best matches contour 1?* (B)

4. Review and clarify all the figures and the concepts depicted by the symbols.

FOLLOW-UP

➤ Have available some clear transparencies, transparency pens or crayons, and Photo 2B (see page 101) or another photo showing a side view of mountains. Have students place clear transparencies over the photo and trace the elevation to produce a cross section of the mountains in the photo.

➤ Have the students prepare contour-line diagrams showing the relative height of the mountains in Photo 2B.

Name _____

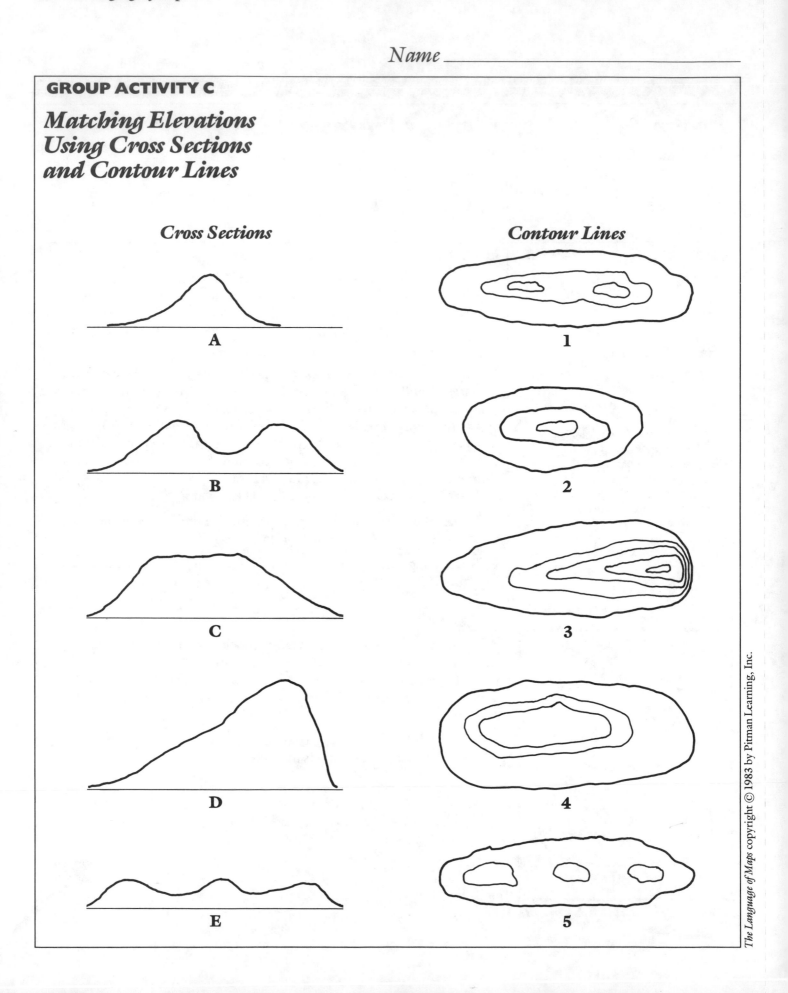

GROUP ACTIVITY C

Matching Elevations Using Cross Sections and Contour Lines

Cross Sections

A

B

C

D

E

Contour Lines

1

2

3

4

5

Lesson 13   *Comparing Size and Shape*

OBJECTIVE

to determine the comparative size and shape of land areas when using maps and a table

PREPARATION

MATERIALS

Maps 3, 4, and 5, transparencies or 24-by-36-inch oaktag copies (see pages 106–108)

Map 2, transparency (see page 105)

Map 17, two transparencies (see page 120); cut apart nations on one transparency

Table 1, 24-by-35-inch copy (see page 30)

overhead projector

clear transparency

world map, wall size or large enough for the entire class to see

TIME

social studies or geography class

LESSON

1. Review the use of symbols for elevation and explain to the students that in this lesson they will read and interpret symbols that show the sizes and shapes of different land areas.

2. **Say:** *The United States has increased in land size over the years. Here is what it looked like in 1789.* Show Map 3. *Here is what it looked like in 1825.* Show Map 4. **Ask:** *How can we tell that the size of the land has increased?* (The map covers a larger area.) *Here is the size of the United States 24 years later.* Show Map 5. *Had it grown in size?* (yes) *Can you guess how much it had grown since 1789?* (approximately double) *In what directions did the United States grow?* (west and south) *How do we know?* (Since there is no directional sign, north is to the top.)

3. Show Map 2 and **say:** *Remember this map? It helped us earlier in finding the high and low elevations of South America. We found that besides showing elevations it shows us boundary lines. What is the symbol for boundary lines?* (a dashed-and-dotted line) *What are boundary lines for?* (so we can tell one country from another) Remind students that maps that show boundary lines are called political maps.

4. Place the transparency of Map 17 showing the boundaries of South American countries over Map 2 and **say:** *Here is the map showing national boundary lines without elevations. Which seems to be the largest country in South America?* (Brazil) *Which seems to be second largest in size?* (Argentina)

5. Place transparency cutouts of each of the other countries from Map 17 over Map 2 and **ask:** *How many countries other than Chile and Argentina do you think it would take to equal the size of Brazil?* Place cutouts of various countries side by side on Brazil, naming each one, until they roughly match Brazil's size. Remove the cutouts.

6. Place a clear transparency over Map 2 and trace only coastlines. **Say:** *We know that the largest countries in area are Brazil and Argentina. Which country has the longest coastline?* (Brazil) *Brazil's coastline is 6,019 miles, and Argentina's is 2,940 miles.*

7. **Ask:** *Which country seems to be the smallest in size?* (French Guiana) *All but two South American nations border on an ocean. Which are the two landlocked nations?* (Bolivia and Paraguay) *Which of those countries is smaller in size?* (Paraguay)

Lesson 13 (continued)

8. **Say:** *Now let's look at the countries of the world that are largest in size.* Display Table 1 and read it aloud as a group. **Ask:** *How are the nations listed?* (alphabetically) *Which nation is the largest?* (U.S.S.R.) *Second largest?* (China) *Smallest?* (India) *Which three countries are closest in size?* (Canada, China, U.S.A.)

9. **Say:** *Let's look at the shapes of some of these countries.* Turn to the world map or to an atlas in the class textbook. *Are any of these countries similar in shape even if they're not similar in size?* (India and Brazil; Australia and China) Ask students to use addition to figure out from Table 1 which country is so large in size that its area exceeds that of three of the other countries combined. (U.S.S.R.) Have the students name the three countries whose areas they added. (any combination of India and two other countries except both China and Canada)

FOLLOW-UP

➤Using Table 1, have students list every combination of three nations and their land areas in comparison with that of the U.S.S.R. After each sum, have the students indicate whether the sum is less than (<) or greater than (>) the area of the U.S.S.R. For example:

Australia	2,967,909	
China	3,691,502	
U.S.A.	3,554,609	U.S.S.R.
	10,214,020 >	8,570,060

➤Place the Map 2 transparency and the transparency cutouts of South American countries at your learning center for students to compare locations, sizes, and shapes of the nations.

TABLE 1 *Land Area of Seven Largest Nations in Size* (in square miles)

Australia	2,967,909
Brazil	3,286,170
Canada	3,621,616
China	3,691,502
India	1,262,274
U.S.A.	3,554,609
U.S.S.R.	8,570,060

Lesson 14 *Using Symbols for Cities*

OBJECTIVE

to use symbols to identify the shapes and sizes of cities when using an aerial photo or a map

PREPARATION

MATERIALS

Photo 3, projection or transparency (see page 102)
Map 6, projection (see page 109)
opaque or overhead projector
clear transparency
transparency pen or crayon

TIME

social studies or geography class

LESSON

1. **Say:** *In the previous lesson we examined the sizes and shapes of countries. Today we're going to examine towns and cities. One way is to compare their sizes and shapes from the air.* Show Photo 3, of the Connecticut River Valley in Massachusetts. *This is a photo taken from a satellite 10,000 feet up, almost two miles above sea level.* Trace the river. *On both sides of this river are towns.* **Ask:** *Where are the two towns?* Trace the shape of each town or have students do it. *Which is larger in size?* (the one at the bottom left of photo, South Deerfield; the other is Sunderland) *How would you describe their shapes?* (rectangular) **Say:** *Towns and cities also may be other shapes, such as circular, square, and triangular. In your free time, look for photos or maps showing shapes of cities.*

2. **Say:** *Today we're going to look at how symbols are used to show sizes of cities in terms of population and area. The shapes we just discussed also may be used to indicate size; for example, we can use a circle. The larger the circle, the larger the city is in area.* Draw three circles of different sizes on the chalkboard and label them A, B, and C. Make circle C largest and circle A smallest. **Ask:** *If each of these circles represents a city, which is the largest city?* (C) *The smallest?* (A) *Is city C the largest in size (or area) or in number of people?* (size or area) *What if we used circles to indicate population? Which city would have the smallest number of people in it?* (A) *Which city would have neither the most nor the fewest people in it?* (B)

3. **Say:** *Find some maps in your social studies book and tell us what other symbols map makers use to show towns or cities.* (dots or points; clusters of dots; clusters of circles; or any combination of dots and circles and different shapes and sizes) Note examples on the chalkboard.

Lesson 14 (continued)

4. Show Map 6 and **ask:** *What country is directly to the south of Canada?* (United States) *How do we know, since this map doesn't show the United States?* (learned it elsewhere; found it on another map) *How do we know that it's south?* (Since there is no directional sign, south is toward the bottom.) *How would you describe where most of these Canadian cities are located?* (near water; along the American border; southern portion of Canada) *What do the symbols in the key represent?* (size of city population) *Which cities have more than 500,000 people?* (Calgary, Winnipeg, Edmonton, Vancouver, Ottawa, Toronto, Montreal, and Quebec) *How do we know?* (first two symbols in the key) *Which city has a population of less than 500,000?* (Halifax) *Which three cities have the most people?* (Montreal, Toronto, Vancouver) *How do we know?* (They are shown with the first symbol in the key.)

FOLLOW-UP

➤ Have the students use their social studies textbooks to find a population map of Canadian cities. On paper, have them write the page and title of the map found. Have them list the population symbols from the key of the map, describing each symbol. Next, have the students indicate how these symbols are similar to or different from those shown in the key of Map 6.

➤ Have students use their social studies books to find a map showing aerial sizes or shapes of Canadian cities. On paper, have them write the page and title of the map found. Have them list the symbols for the different shapes and sizes of Canadian cities. Next, have the students describe each shape or size in geometric terms, for example, "seems more rectangular."

Location and Distance

| **Lesson 15** | **Determining Directions and Distance on a Floor Plan** |

OBJECTIVE

to identify directions and determine distance in the classroom and on a floor plan

PREPARATION

Note: Arrange desks or tables in the classroom to create aisles representing streets and roads as in Map 7 (see page 110). You may wish to modify the map to approximate the street or road grid system of your school community.

MATERIALS
floor plan of your classroom on a 5-by-10-foot sheet of butcher paper (see Map 7)
pen or crayon

TIME
social studies class

LESSON

1. Explain that the room is arranged to represent a part of the school neighborhood or a map, which you will show later, and that the aisles represent streets.

2. Have students identify the main and intermediate directions by use of the sun, landmarks, or a compass so that the class will know the direction (cardinal and left or right) of each aisle (street). Quiz orally to reinforce directions of streets.

3. Place the floor plan or a map similar to Map 7 on the floor or on a set of desks. Have students orient the map to the room and indicate all four directions on the map.

4. Identify each set of desks as a block or a mile and have students determine how far they could travel in any given direction.

5. Clarify and summarize concepts related to the lesson.

FOLLOW-UP

➤ If your school is in a city or town and you used blocks for distance, have the students imagine they are in a rural area. Refer to the distance between aisles as a mile and determine the distance of a given direction. Do the opposite if you are located in a rural area.

Lesson 16

Finding Our Way around Classville

OBJECTIVE

to locate places and compute distances in a simulation game in which aisles are streets or roads and desks and tables are houses or buildings

PREPARATION

Note: The purpose of this game is to help students locate places in space using distance and direction. Keep the room arranged as in the preceding lesson, with the same classroom or spatial grid system and directions. Next, label the aisles as roads (if a rural area) or streets (if a town, city, or urban area) by printing the names of the roads or streets on manila strips and placing each label in the appropriate aisle.

MATERIALS

Map 7 (see page 110) or variation, with names of real streets or roads and directions indicated, or Map 8, a 5-by-10-foot copy, if using an imaginary place (see page 111)

manila strips, 4 inches by 18 inches

Map 7 or 8, Figure 7 (see below), and blank paper for each student for follow-up

TIME

social studies class

LESSON

1. **Say:** *Today we're going to play a game called Finding Our Way around Classville. Let's put out our street signs.* Call on students to identify the names on the signs and to place each sign in the correct aisle of either Map 7 or 8.

2. Review cardinal directions with the class. Then **say:** *I'll call on one of you and ask you to visit someone. You must show us the shortest way to get there. As you travel, tell us: (1) what direction you are going; (2) whether you turn left or right; and (3) the number of blocks it is to where you are going.* Write the steps on the chalkboard or on a chart for the class to see.

3. Call on one student. Tell him or her to visit another resident of Classville that you choose. Have both stand for everyone to see.

4. Give the visitor a few seconds to plan the shortest route; then tell him or her to begin, naming cardinal directions, left and right turns, and distance as he or she walks.

5. Have the visitor return home, again noting directions, turns, and distance. Point out that the distance doesn't change, but the cardinal directions and the turns are reversed.

6. Repeat the game with other students. When they are in doubt about the shortest route, have them try different routes until the shortest one is found.

FOLLOW-UP

➤ Play the game as above, this time having two students at the chalkboard to record the data as in Figure 7 below. In each instance, the student must summarize her or his travel. For example, Chris would say: "I turned right and went east two blocks, then I turned left and went north three blocks. It was five blocks to Juan's place."

FIGURE 7 *Steps in Classville Game*

	LEFT/RIGHT	DIRECTION	DISTANCE
CHRIS	right	east	2 blocks
	left	north	3 blocks

Lesson 16 *(continued)*

➤ Distribute copies of Map 7 or 8 and blank paper to each student to play the game silently. Repeat the above procedure in a simulation game, calling on one student to visit another, only this time have the student make the trip using the map instead of actually walking from place to place. After you announce each visit, have the students record the visitor's name on blank paper and write the directions, turns, and distance as they did aloud before. After all silent visits are completed, have each student report his or her journey to the class, noting destination, directions, and distance, and have recorders complete the data as in Figure 7.

Lesson 17

Using an Imaginary Neighborhood Map

OBJECTIVE

to read and interpret comparative locations and distances on a neighborhood map

PREPARATION

MATERIALS
Map 8, transparency, and copy for each student (see page 111)
blank paper for each student
overhead projector
transparency pen or crayon

TIME
social studies class

LESSON

1. Distribute Map 8 and have the students write their names on paper.

2. Project Map 8. **Ask:** *What is the symbol for a school?* (building with pointed roof and flag) *On what street is a school?* (Daring Street) *Between what streets is it located?* (Third and Fourth avenues) *What is the symbol for a house?* (square) *Where is house 1 located?* (Baker Street, between Second and Third avenues) *How do we know it is house 1?* (matches square under key and has *1* in square) *Where is house 2 located on the map?* (Second Avenue, between Daring and Easter streets) *Give directions for the shortest route from house 1 to the school.* (east ½ block, south 2 blocks, east ½ block) *How many blocks long is the shortest route?* (3) *Give directions for the shortest route from the school to house 2.* (west 1½ blocks, south ½ block) *How many blocks long is the shortest route?* (2) *Which house is closer to the school?* (2) *On which street must a person walk to get from house 1 or 2 to the school the shortest way?* (Daring Street)

FOLLOW-UP

➤ Have the students add other symbols to the map and create route and distance questions for each other.

Lesson 18

Doing Field Work — Walking a Mile

OBJECTIVE

to note time in relation to distance under varying circumstances, and to note observations

PREPARATION

Note: Prior to this lesson, determine an itinerary for a field trip, including time of day, distance, and route. Also, plan on taking a first aid kit, a compass, a direction chart (if students are unsure of directions in the neighborhood), a camera, a sketch pad, and any other necessary materials. You may wish to make a map of the area around your school and trace the route of your walk on it before the trip.

MATERIALS
Chart 7, copied on chalkboard or 24-by-36-inch oaktag (see below)

TIME
social studies class

OBSERVATION GUIDELINES

1. Note what directions we took.
2. Note whose houses we saw along the way.
3. Note what stores or buildings we saw as we walked.
4. Note what new buildings were being constructed.
5. Note any other landmarks we saw that we thought were important.

CHART 7

LESSON

1. **Say:** *Today we will see how long it takes to walk a mile and to do the five things on our Observation Guidelines.* Show Chart 7. Have the class read the chart aloud, and clarify each point for them. Pass out pads and pencils and explain to the students that they will use them to sketch and list what they observe. As you leave, note the time on the chalkboard.

2. As the class walks, have students determine directions using whatever means are available, such as the sun, a compass, or a map. Remind the students to note distances in blocks and all changes of direction. Also remind them to note other phenomena listed on the guidelines. Stop frequently to allow time for writing and sketching observations.

3. Upon returning to the classroom, record the time on the chalkboard. Compute the time it took to walk a mile.

4. Have students report their findings orally for each item listed on Chart 7. Record their findings on the chalkboard. Have students share their sketches.

5. At another time, walk the same route again without stopping to make observations. Note the starting and finishing times on the chalkboard and compute the time spent walking. Discuss the differences between the two walks. **Ask:** *How long would it take to ride the route on a bike? In a car?* Have the students discuss their answers.

FOLLOW-UP

➤Suggest that students illustrate, list, write a story or poem about, or map their observations during the walks.

➤Suggest to the class that if they have a chance to ride in a car, they should note how long it takes to ride one mile in any of the following places or situations: their neighborhood; downtown; near a shopping center; on the highway; on the freeway (or expressway or parkway) during normal traffic and again during the morning or afternoon rush hour.

Lesson 19

Using Landmarks as Symbols

OBJECTIVE

to identify and use landmarks in locating places and following routes of travel on a neighborhood map

PREPARATION

Note: Have your neighborhood map oriented on the floor or pinned on a wall, and have Map 8 ready for projection.

MATERIALS
neighborhood map
Map 8, transparency (see page 111)
overhead projector
transparency pen or crayon
blank paper for each student for
    follow-up

TIME
social studies class

LESSON

1. Use the second follow-up activity in the preceding lesson as the basis for a discussion on comparing and contrasting the varying amounts of time it takes to go the same distance in different places or at different times of the day.

2. Plot appropriate routes and distances on the neighborhood map.

3. **Ask:** *During our walk or during your ride in the car, how many of you used a landmark such as a store, a church, a gas station, or an empty lot to figure out the distance? You may remember that some of us used a landmark such as a gas station to know that we were to turn in a particular direction at that point on our trip. So, a landmark may be anything we can use to note where a place is, where to turn, or how far away a place is. What landmark did you use? Where is it on the map?* Plot some of the landmarks students identify and locate.

4. **Say:** *Let's look at the map of an imaginary neighborhood.* Project Map 8. **Ask:** *If we were going the shortest route from house 1 to house 2, what landmark would we pass?* (gas station) *From the school, what landmark would we pass to take the shortest route to either house?* (store)

FOLLOW-UP

➤ Distribute blank paper to each student. Have each student write his or her name on the paper and list and draw at least five landmarks he or she found or used in the walk or ride. Then have the students write how they used each landmark in finding their way. Discuss their uses of landmarks.

Lesson 20 — Using Line Segments or Arcs to Visualize

OBJECTIVE

to plot three cities and estimate distance in terms of air miles and time using line segments or arcs as the route of travel

PREPARATION

Note: An air atlas from a major airline would be helpful in determining the mileage between cities in the activities in this lesson.

MATERIALS

Map 9, copy for each student, and transparency for Group Activity F (see page 112)
Group Activities D, E, and F (see pages 42 and 43)
Figures 8 and 9 (see page 41)
pencil and two sheets of paper for each student
overhead projector
blank transparencies
transparency pen or crayon

NEW TERMS
arcs
line segments
relative distance
relative location

TIME
social studies class

LESSON

1. Review and summarize uses of points of reference, especially landmarks (trees, lots, signs, buildings, and so forth), and how they help us determine directions and distance.

2. **Say:** *Today, we're going to use points and* **line segments,** *or* **arcs.** *For example, if you lived in Paris, France, and were going to Frankfurt, West Germany, you would place a point, or dot, on the left side of your paper with a P for* Frankfurt, Paris *alongside it.* Show on the chalkboard. *On the other side, using an F for* Frankfurt, *you would place another dot.* Show on the chalkboard.

•F

P •

Next, you would connect the two points with a line segment, or straight line, as if you were thinking of this area as a flat map. Connect the two points with a straight line. *However, if you were picturing Paris and Frankfurt on a globe, you might connect the two with an arc, or curved line, like this.* Show on the chalkboard.

Either way is correct. In both cases we will be approximating location and distance. We are not trying to locate places exactly, nor are we trying to determine distances exactly. We are going to work with what is called **relative location** *and* **relative distance.** *Location and distance in this instance are relative in that we are determining approximately, not exactly, where each place is located and about how far apart they are.* You may want to repeat this procedure using different, more familiar cities until students feel comfortable doing it.

3. Distribute blank sheets of paper to the class. Have the students place their papers sideways on their desks. Lead the students in Group Activity D.

4. Have the class turn their papers over and give directions for Group Activity E.

Lesson 20 (continued)

5. Distribute a second sheet of paper to each student and give directions for Group Activity F.

6. Review and summarize.

FOLLOW-UP

➤ Try other combinations of cities appropriate to where you live. Use the format of Group Activities D and E to compare air miles and air time.

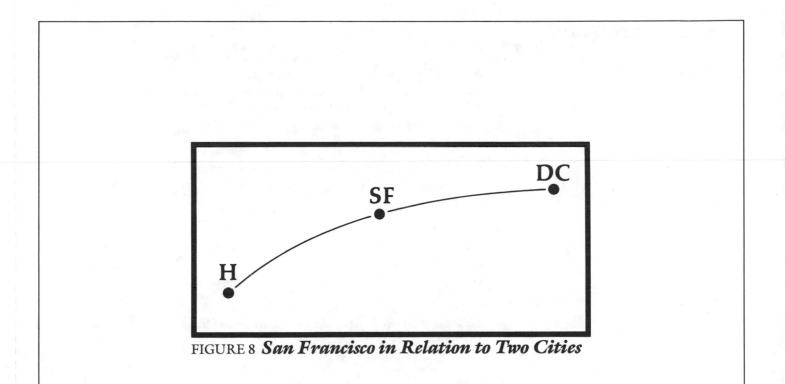

FIGURE 8 *San Francisco in Relation to Two Cities*

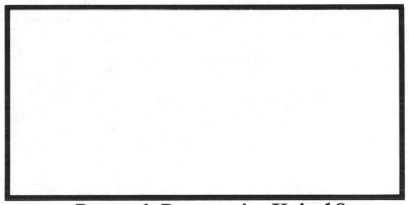

FIGURE 9 *Rectangle Representing United States*

GROUP ACTIVITY D

Comparing Distances in Air Miles

1. **Say:** *Imagine that this blank sheet of paper is a map of the United States, including Hawaii and Alaska. On one side of your map, place a dot with the letter H, indicating Honolulu. On the opposite side of the paper, place another point, this one for Washington, D.C., with DC to identify it. Connect the two points with an arc or a line segment.*

2. **Say:** *You are taking an air flight from Honolulu to Washington, D.C., with a stopover at San Francisco. In terms of distance in air miles, plot San Francisco as a point on the arc or line segment on your paper. Label this point SF.*

3. After everyone has finished, **ask:** *To which city does San Francisco appear closer?* Await answers without prompting. **Ask:** *In air miles, to which city do you think San Francisco is closer?* Receive and compare findings. (Actual mileage according to one major airline: SF– H, 2,400 miles; SF– DC, 2,417 miles)

4. Discuss an appropriate title for the map and have the students write the title and the date on their maps.

GROUP ACTIVITY E

Comparing Distances through Time in Flight

1. **Say:** *Repeat the procedures in Group Activity D, this time considering time in flight between Honolulu and San Francisco and between San Francisco and Washington, D.C.* (approximately five hours each flight)

2. Compare findings with those found in Group Activity D.

GROUP ACTIVITY F

Comparing a Rectangle with an Outline Map

1. **Say:** *On your paper, sketch a rectangle that is wider than it is tall.* Show Figure 9. *Picture the rectangle as the United States without Hawaii and Alaska. On one side, show New York as a point. Identify it as NY. At the other side of the rectangle, plot San Francisco as a point. Identify it as SF. Connect the points with an arc or a line segment. In terms of air miles, plot Chicago with a dot on the arc or line segment. Identify Chicago with the letter C.*

2. Distribute Map 9 to the students and repeat step 1 above.

3. After everyone has finished, **ask:** *Which was easier to work with, the rectangle or the outline map?* (map) *Why?* (The Great Lakes helped in locating Chicago.)

4. Compare and correct student plottings in both the rectangle and outline maps.

5. **Ask:** *To which city is Chicago closer in distance?* (New York) *In time?* (New York)

Lesson 21

Comparing Distances Using Two Maps

OBJECTIVE

to compare and determine relative distances between cities on two maps using directions and scale

PREPARATION

Note: We are again dealing with air miles in relative terms. Actual air distances involve national and international regulations, and the route between two places may not be a direct line between the two points. Land distances (via highways and roads) may differ considerably from air distances. Also, we need to be aware that a map distorts true distance and true direction; map distances are approximations when we use a ruler to find the distance between two points. On the ground, actual distance is affected by land barriers, natural and artificial.

MATERIALS

Maps 6 and 10, transparencies, and copy for each student (see pages 109 and 113)
ruler for each student
overhead projector
transparency pen or crayon

TIME

social studies class

LESSON

1. **Say:** *In the last lesson we plotted cities and determined the distances between them. Today we are going to find the distances on two maps that have the cities already plotted for us.* Distribute Maps 6 and 10 to the class and project Map 6.

2. **Ask:** *What is the title of Map 6?* (Populations of Canadian Cities) *How many symbols are there in the key?* (3) *Which way is north on this map?* (toward the top of the page) *How do we know?* (no directional sign given) *Where are most of the cities?* (in the south)

3. **Say:** *Let's look at Map 10.* Project Map 10 and **ask:** *What is the title of Map 10?* (Some Major Canadian Cities) *How many symbols are there in the key?* (3, including the directional sign) *Where is north on this map?* (top) *How do we know?* (directional sign) *How is Map 10 like Map 6?* (It is a map of Canada; it has a title and a key.) *How are the maps different?* (Give clues to obtain these answers: Map 6 shows scale populations of cities, while Map 10 only identifies the cities; Map 10 indicates scale and north, while Map 6 indicates neither; Map 6 is about half the size of Map 10 yet covers the same area.) *Which Canadian city shown on the maps is the farthest north?* (Edmonton) *Farthest south?* (Toronto) *Farthest west?* (Vancouver) *Farthest east?* (Halifax)

4. Project Map 6 and **say:** *Look again at Map 6. Which city appears closer to Calgary—Vancouver or Winnipeg?* (Vancouver) *Which city appears farther from Montreal—Winnipeg or Halifax?* (Winnipeg) *Which city is farthest from Ottawa—Quebec, Halifax, or Toronto?* (Halifax)

5. Project Map 10 and **say:** *Let's look again at Map 10. How can this map help us to see if we were right in our answers to the questions I asked about Map 6?* (the scale) Point out that there are three ways to show scale—with words (as on the map), as a ratio (1 inch: 300 miles), or graphically:

0   150   300

Lesson 21 (continued)

6. Have the students use rulers to find the distances between the following cities on Map 10: Calgary and Vancouver (**450 miles**); Calgary and Winnipeg (**750 miles**); Montreal and Winnipeg (**1,113 miles**); Montreal and Halifax (**525 miles**).

FOLLOW-UP

➤ Have students look through their social studies textbooks to find maps with and without scales. Have them identify, on paper, one of each and have them explain how to tell distance on each map.

Inferential Reading

Lesson 22   *Using Road Signs*

OBJECTIVE

to determine exact and relative distances using road signs

PREPARATION

Note: Determine whether you will teach the lesson in terms of miles or kilometers and prepare the lesson accordingly.

MATERIALS
Figures 10 and 11, charts or
   transparencies (see page 48)
overhead projector
transparency pen or crayon

TIME
social studies class

LESSON

1. **Say:** *Earlier, we used landmarks to find our way. Today, we are going to use road signs to determine how far an imaginary place is. These road signs list distance in miles (or kilometers). The cities on each road sign are listed in order from nearest to farthest.*

2. **Say:** *Let's look at the first road sign and read each place and the distance together.* Show Figure 10. Have the students read the names and distances aloud as a group.

3. To teach the concept of exact distance, **ask:** *How far is it from here to Collar?* (1 mile or kilometer) *How far is it from here to Eastly?* (5 miles or kilometers) *How far is it from here to Kent?* (10 miles or kilometers) *How far is it from Collar to Eastly?* (4 miles or kilometers) *How far is it from Eastly to Kent?* (5 miles or kilometers) *How far is it from Collar to Kent?* (9 miles or kilometers)

4. To teach the concept of relative distance, **ask:** *Which town is nearest to us?* (Collar) *Farthest?* (Kent) *Which town is in between, that is, neither nearest nor farthest?* (Eastly)

5. Show Figure 11 and have the students read it aloud as a group. Returning to the concept of exact distance, **ask:** *How far is it from Durkin to here?* (10 miles or kilometers) *How far is it from Molar to here?* (20 miles or kilometers) *How far is it from Pint to here?* (50 miles or kilometers) *How far is it from Sole to here?* (100 miles or kilometers) *How far is it from Durkin to Molar?* (10 miles or kilometers) *From Molar to Pint?* (30 miles or kilometers) *From Pint to Sole?* (50 miles or kilometers)

6. Mixing the concepts of exact and relative distances, **ask:** *Which city is the farthest from us?* (Sole) *Which city is 50 miles from us?* (Pint) *Which city is the closest to us?* (Durkin) *Which city is 20 miles from us?* (Molar)

7. To reinforce the concept of relative distance, **ask:** *Which city is midway between Sole and us?* (Pint) *Which city is closer to Molar —Durkin or Pint?* (Durkin) *Which city is closer to Pint —Molar or Sole?* (Molar) *Which city is farther from Pint —Durkin or Sole?* (Sole) *Which city is closest to Pint —Durkin, Molar, or Sole?* (Molar) Have the students explain how they determined the answers.

Lesson 22 (continued)

FOLLOW-UP

➤ Have the students select towns or cities on a road map. Have the students write the names of the cities or towns and make road signs that include at least three other towns. Next, have the students write questions involving exact distance, relative distance, and both.

Road Signs

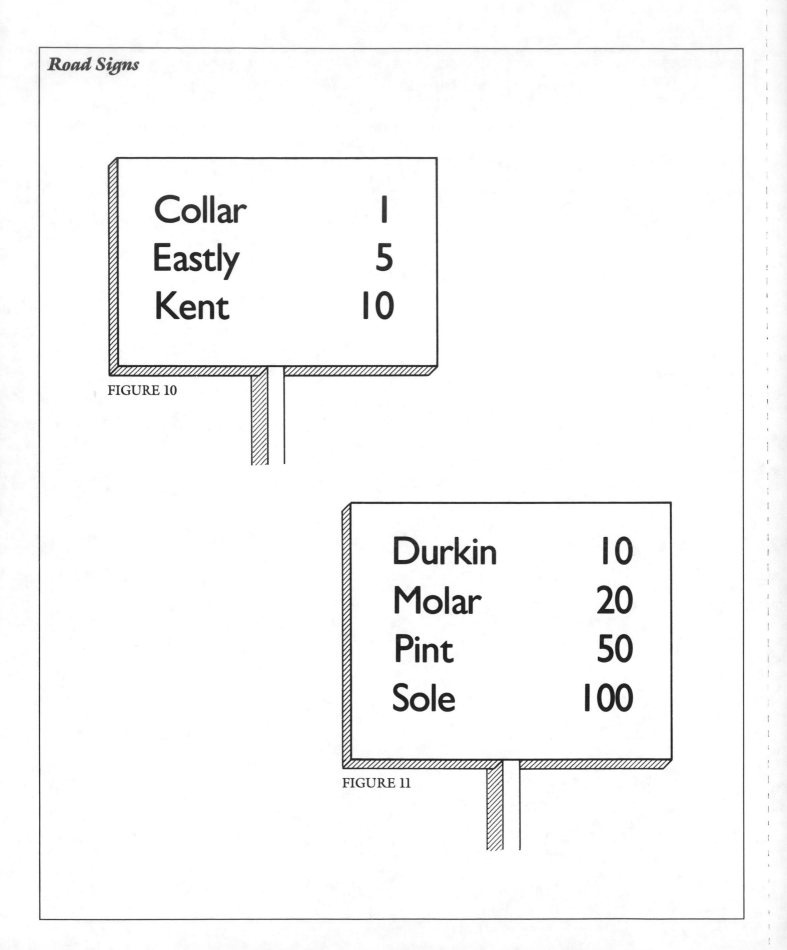

FIGURE 10

Collar	1
Eastly	5
Kent	10

FIGURE 11

Durkin	10
Molar	20
Pint	50
Sole	100

Lesson 23

Comparing Distances Using Road Signs

OBJECTIVE

to compare distances between places using road signs

PREPARATION

MATERIALS
Figures 10 and 11, transparencies or charts (see page 48)
road sign of local area, similar to Figures 10 and 11

TIME
social studies class

LESSON

1. **Say:** *We have been reading road signs as landmarks. How have they helped us?* Have the students discuss their answers.

2. **Say:** *Today, we are going to use these road signs again, but in a different way. Let's first look at the one that shows that Collar is one mile (or kilometer) away from us.* Show Figure 10 and **ask:** *If Collar is one mile away, how many times farther away is Eastly?* (5) *How many times farther away than Collar is Kent?* (10)

3. **Say:** *Now, let's do the same with this road sign.* Show Figure 11. *If Durkin is 10 miles away, how many times farther away is Molar?* (2) *Pint?* (5) *Sole?* (10) *Now, let's look at this road sign of our area. Let's name a place nearby and say how far it is. Now name a place farther away and tell how many times farther it is. For example, let's say that Modesto is 15 miles from Turlock and San Francisco is 105 miles from Turlock. San Francisco is seven times farther away from Turlock than Modesto.*

FOLLOW-UP

➤ Have the students make up their own road signs similar to Figures 10 and 11. Have students identify exact distances on their road signs by reading each place and distance aloud.

➤ Have the students ask each other questions about relative distances of places on maps that they show to the class. Have the students report aloud relative distances of specific towns and cities on the maps.

Lesson 24

Interpreting a Road Map

OBJECTIVE

to read a road map inferentially using map skills learned thus far

PREPARATION

Note: To simplify the odd/even highway-numbering concept, you may wish to color the odd-numbered and the even-numbered highways differently. (Some duplicating procedures duplicate colors.) Coloring can help students visualize the distinctions more readily.

MATERIALS
Map 11, transparency, and copy
  for each student (see page 114)
Figure 12, transparency or chart (see
  page 51)
overhead projector
transparency pen or crayon

TIME
social studies class

LESSON

1. Distribute copies of Map 11 to the class and project the map. **Say:** *This is part of a road map of an imaginary place. There are several symbols in the key. First, we are going to use the key to see how highways are numbered.*

2. **Ask:** *In which directions do Highways 7 and 67 go?* (north and south) *In which direction does State Highway 9 go?* (north and south) *Are these odd-numbered or even-numbered highways?* (odd-numbered) *In which direction, then, do odd-numbered highways go?* (north and south) *In which direction do you think even-numbered ones will go?* Obtain inferences. *Let's see!*

3. **Ask:** *In which direction does U.S. Highway 16 go?* (east and west) *State Highway 8?* (east and west) *U.S. Highway 32?* (east and west) *Were we right about even-numbered highways? Why? What, then, can we say about highway numbers and highways?* (Odd-numbered highways go north and south; even-numbered highways go east and west.)

4. **Say:** *Now we are going to look at two more symbols. What kinds of roads do we find on this map?* (paved and graveled) *Which highway is both paved and graveled?* (State Highway 9) *On which kind of road is it easier to ride or drive a car?* (paved) Have the students explain their answers.

5. **Say:** *Three highways cross a river. Which highways are they?* (State Highways 7, 8, and 9) *If you were riding in a car on any of these highways, what would you need to go over to cross the river?* (bridge) *How do we know it is a bridge?* (key) *How do we know which symbol is the river?* (key)

6. **Say:** *U.S. Highways 32 and 67 go through the same city. How do we know what a city is?* (key) *What is the name of the city the highways go through?* (Front) *U.S. Highways 32 and 67 both end at a city or a town. Which highway ends at a city?* (U.S. Highway 67) *What is the name of the city?* (Cushing) *Which highway ends at a town?* (U.S. Highway 32) *What is the name of the town?* (Alma)

7. **Ask:** *Which U.S. highway goes through two towns?* (U.S. Highway 16) *What are the names of the towns?* (Ash and Box) *Which state highway goes through two towns, crossing a bridge in between them?* (State Highway 9) *What are the names of the towns?* (Delta and Alma)

Lesson 24 (continued)

8. **Ask:** *If we took State Highway 9 to U.S. Highway 16, in what direction would we be going?* (north) *When we reached U.S. Highway 16, in what direction would we need to go to reach Box?* (west)

9. **Say:** *Notice the numbers along the roads and highways. Each number tells us how many miles it is between two points, usually towns, cities, or intersections of highways. For example, notice the number 12 alongside the road between Delta and U.S. Highway 16. That means it's 12 miles between the town of Delta and U.S. Highway 16. Now that we've reached U.S. Highway 16, how far is it to Box?* (6 miles) *How do we know?* (Distance is indicated on the map.)

10. **Say:** *Let's find the town of Helen on the map. Which is the shorter route from Helen to Cushing —through Delta or through Front?* (through Front) *How do we know?* (It's 16 miles to delta plus 15 miles to Cushing, for a total of 31 miles; it's 14 miles to Front, plus 5 miles to Eli, plus 10 miles to Cushing, for a total of 29 miles) *Which two communities on the map are closest to each other in road miles?* (Eli and Front)

11. Show Figure 12 and **ask:** *Where would this sign be placed?* (at Delta) *How do we know?* (Delta is 16 miles from Helen and 12 miles from U.S. Highway 16.) *What did we have to know to answer the questions about this map?* (Give clues to obtain answers that include the following: symbols in the key and road map; location of symbols on the map; directions; and distance noted along roads and highways.) **Ask:** *What did we have to do to answer the questions about this map?* (Give clues to obtain answers that include the following: trace routes using directions, road signs, and highway and road symbols; and determine distance in terms of indications along roads and highways.) Point out to the students that in this lesson they used every map concept and skill that they have learned thus far.

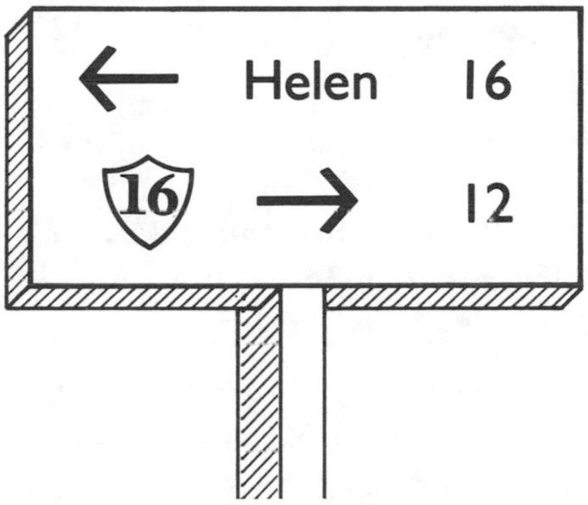

FIGURE 12 **Road Sign**

FOLLOW-UP

➤ Have students prepare additional road signs and questions regarding Map 11 to share and solve with the class.

Lesson 25   *Using Two Maps to Gather Data*

OBJECTIVE

to draw conclusions regarding location of cities by relating and inferring data from two different types of maps—physical and political

PREPARATION

MATERIALS
Maps 12 and 13, one copy for each pair of students (see pages 115 and 116)

Maps 2, 10, 12, and 13, transparencies (see pages 105, 113, 115, and 116)

overhead projector

transparency pen or crayon

Group Activity G, one copy for each pair of students (see page 54)

TIME
social studies class

LESSON

1. Divide the class into teams of two and distribute Map 12 to each team. Show Map 12 and **say:** *In the last lesson we read and interpreted part of a road map. Today we will examine two different types of maps.*

2. **Ask:** *What is the title of Map 12?* (Physical Map of North America) *What do we mean by a physical map?* (one that shows physical features) *How do we know directions on this map?* (The North Pole is indicated.) *What symbols are shown in the key?* (scale, rivers, mountains, plains)

3. Show Map 10. **Ask:** *How is this scale different from the scale on Map 12?* (The scale on Map 10 uses words and numbers; the scale on Map 12 uses a line with marks and numbers.)

4. Show Map 2. **Ask:** *How is Map 12 different from Map 2?* (Map 12 is of North America; Map 2 is of South America. Map 12 shows only mountains and plains or lowlands; Map 2 shows mountains, lowlands or plains, plateaus, hills, and national boundaries. Map 2 does not show a scale.) *How are Maps 2 and 12 alike?* (Both are physical maps.)

5. **Say:** *Let's look again at Map 12. Where do we find the greatest elevation?* (in the west) *How do we know that it's the west?* (The North Pole is at the top of the map.) *Where else is there a mountainous area?* (in the east) *Where do we find plains or lowlands along the coast or shore?* (Pacific and Atlantic oceans, Gulf of Mexico, Hudson Bay, and Beaufort and Bering seas) *What is the land like in central North America?* (lowlands or plains) You may want to tell the students that this area is called the Great Plains. *What can we say about the mountainous area along the western part of North America?* (It is continuous; it looks like it continues into South America.) You may want to show Map 2 to follow the continuity into the Andean range.

6. Show Map 13 and **say:** *We've been looking at a physical map of North America. What kind of map is this one?* (political) *You remember that a physical map shows the relief of the land—its elevation or lack of it. A political map shows us states (or provinces) or countries by using boundary lines.*

7. Distribute a copy of Map 13 to each pair of students and **ask:** *How can we tell directions?* (The North Pole is indicated.) *How many symbols are there on the map?* (5) *What are they?* (scale, national boundaries, national capitals, cities, rivers) *Which symbols are found on both Map 12 and Map 13?* (rivers and scale)

Lesson 25 *(continued)*	8. **Say:** *Have both maps in front of you. You will need to examine both maps to answer most of the following questions.* **Ask:** *Which city is an inland city in the mountainous region of Canada?* (Edmonton) *Of the United States?* (Denver) *Of Mexico?* (Mexico City) *Which city is located in the Canadian plains?* (Winnipeg) *American plains?* (Kansas City) *Which cities in the western United States are seaports?* (San Francisco and Los Angeles) *Which two North American cities are lake ports?* (Toronto and Chicago) *Which North American city is located in the plains or lowlands near the Atlantic coast?* (Washington, D.C.) *Which North American city is located on the Atlantic coast?* (New York) *Where are most of the western cities in North America located?* (near water) *Where are most of the eastern cities in North America located?* (near water) *Where are most of the inland cities of North America located?* (in the Great Plains or near water) *Of the three national capitals shown, which one is an inland city surrounded by mountains?* (Mexico City) *Using both maps, describe Mexico.* (mostly mountainous except along the coasts and the Gulf of Mexico)

FOLLOW-UP

➤ Distribute Group Activity G to each pair of students. Read the title and the directions aloud. Have each pair write their names on the paper and use Maps 12 and 13 to find the answers. Do the activity aloud with students who have difficulty with it.

➤ Have pairs of students report their answers aloud to the class. The answers are:
1. Mexico City
2. Vancouver, San Francisco, Los Angeles, Acapulco, New York, Washington, D.C.
3. Winnipeg, Chicago, Toronto
4. Edmonton, Kansas City, Denver, Ottawa
5. in the mountains or near the ocean
6. in the plains or near lakes
7. near the ocean, lakes, or rivers

➤ **Ask:** *What did we find out about cities and water in North America?* (Most cities are located near water.) Have the students examine social studies textbooks for other political-physical maps to learn about the relationship between cities and water in other areas of the world. Have the students discuss their findings.

Name _____

GROUP ACTIVITY G

*Drawing
Conclusions
from Two Maps*

Directions: Use Maps 12 and 13 to answer the questions below.

1. Which North American capital city is not located near water?

   _____

2. Which six cities are near or along oceans?

   _____   _____

   _____   _____

   _____   _____

3. Which three cities are near or along lakes?

   _____   _____   _____

4. Which four cities are located near or along rivers?

   _____   _____

   _____   _____

5. In the western part of North America, where do the cities seem to be located?

   _____

6. In the central part of North America, where do the cities seem to be located?

   _____

7. In the eastern part of North America, where do the cities seem to be located?

   _____

PART II

Self-Directed Activities

Name _____

Activity 1 — Orienting Myself with the Sun, Shadows, and a Compass: A PUZZLE

Many of the words in this puzzle are map and geography words. Complete the criss-cross puzzle below by filling in words from the list. The words go from left to right or from top to bottom. Put a check next to each word in the list as you use it. AFTERNOON and HUGE have been filled in for you.

✓ AFTERNOON
AM
COMPASS
DIRECTION
EAST
FROM
GALE
GAP
HERE
HOUR
✓ HUGE
INDOOR
IT
MAGNETIC
MAGNETS
MORNING
MY
NEEDLES
NORTH
ON
OUTDOOR
POINT
RIA
SHADOWS
SOS
SOUTH
SUN
TIE
TO
WEST
YARDSTICK

Name _____

Activity 2 Recalling and Drawing Conclusions

Circle the letter of the word or phrase that best completes each sentence.

1. On a sunny day at noon, you can use your shadow to tell which way north is by _____ .
   a. looking at the sun
   b. putting your back to the sun
   c. pointing to the right
   d. pointing to the left

2. If it is a cloudy day, you can tell directions by using _____ .
   a. a compass   c. neither
   b. your shadow   d. either

3. The compass needle or arrow always points _____ .
   a. north   c. east
   b. south   d. west

4. The symbol NW means that the direction is between _____ .
   a. north and south   c. north and east
   b. east and west   d. north and west

5. The symbol SE means that the direction is between _____ .
   a. south and north   c. south and east
   b. west and east   d. south and west

6. The direction southwest is the opposite direction of _____ .
   a. northwest   c. southeast
   b. northeast   d. none of the above

7. The direction northwest is the opposite direction of _____ .
   a. southwest   c. southeast
   b. northeast   d. none of the above

8. The main directions also are called _____ .
   a. imperial directions
   b. intermediate directions
   c. cardinal directions
   d. none of the above

9. The in-between directions also are called _____ .
   a. imperial directions
   b. intermediate directions
   c. cardinal directions
   d. all of the above

10. An in-between direction is a direction between _____ .
    a. the earth and the sun
    b. the earth and the moon
    c. north and east
    d. a freeway and an expressway

11. A _____ will give you correct directions whether it is day or night.
    a. compass   c. sun
    b. shadow   d. moon

12. On a map, a compass rose is used to show _____ .
    a. places   c. signs
    b. roads   d. directions

Name _____

13. Directions on a map sometimes are shown with _____ .
    a. words
    b. lines
    c. a combination of words and lines
    d. all of the above

14. Directional signs may indicate _____ .
    a. cardinal or intermediate directions
    b. the route to take along a street, road, or highway
    c. both
    d. neither

15. When no directional sign is shown on a map, north is _____ .
    a. toward the left
    b. toward the right
    c. toward the top
    d. toward the bottom

Name _____

Activity 3 Finding My Way in North America

Using Map 13, circle the letter of the word that best completes each of the following sentences.

1. The United States is _____ of Mexico.
   - a. north
   - b. south
   - c. east
   - d. west

2. The United States is _____ of Canada.
   - a. north
   - b. south
   - c. east
   - d. west

3. Canada is _____ of Mexico.
   - a. north
   - b. south
   - c. east
   - d. west

4. The Colorado River is _____ of Mexico.
   - a. north
   - b. south
   - c. east
   - d. west

5. The Missouri River is _____ of the Arkansas River.
   - a. north
   - b. south
   - c. east
   - d. west

6. The Columbia River is _____ of the Yukon River.
   - a. northeast
   - b. northwest
   - c. southeast
   - d. southwest

7. The Mississippi River flows from north to _____ .
   - a. north
   - b. south
   - c. east
   - d. west

8. The Rio Grande flows from north to _____ .
   - a. northwest
   - b. southwest
   - c. northeast
   - d. southeast

9. The Mackenzie River flows to the _____ coast.
   - a. north
   - b. south
   - c. east
   - d. west

10. The Columbia River ends at the _____ coast.
    - a. north
    - b. south
    - c. east
    - d. west

11. The Ohio River flows _____ into the Mississippi River.
    - a. south
    - b. southwest
    - c. north
    - d. northeast

12. The St. Lawrence River flows to the _____ coast.
    - a. northeast
    - b. northwest
    - c. southeast
    - d. southwest

13. Cuba is _____ of the United States.
    - a. north
    - b. south
    - c. east
    - d. west

14. Cuba is _____ of Haiti.
    - a. north
    - b. south
    - c. east
    - d. west

15. Washington, D.C., is _____ of Mexico City.
    - a. northeast
    - b. northwest
    - c. southeast
    - d. southwest

Name _____

Activity 4 **Finding My Way with the Compass Rose**

Can you find your way in this puzzle? The map words in the list on this page are all hidden somewhere inside the compass rose. Some words go from left to right, some go from top to bottom, and some go diagonally. Each time you find a word, circle it in the puzzle and make a check next to it on the list. The word BAY has been done for you.

✓ BAY	EASTERN	SCALE
CANADA	FROM	SOUTH
COAST	ISLANDS	SOUTHERN
COLOMBIA	KEY	SUN
COLORADO	MAP	TO
COMPASS	MEXICO	UNITED STATES
CUBA	MILE	UP
DIRECTIONS	NORTH	WATER
DOWN	OCEAN	WEST
EAST	RIVER	WESTERN

The Language of Maps copyright © 1983 by Pitman Learning, Inc.

Name _____

Activity 4 (continued)

U	E	W	E	S	T	E	R	N	S	A	E
N	N	E	Z	O	C	E	A	N	O	C	D
D	X	I	S	L	A	N	D	S	U	O	I
E	O	S	T	G	D	U	U	O	T	L	R
C	Z	W	C	E	T	P	Z	U	H	O	E
O	C	A	N	A	D	A	S	T	E	R	C
L	I	T	Y	M	L	S	X	H	R	A	T
O	W	E	S	T	U	E	T	S	N	D	I
M	F	R	O	M	C	U	B	A	K	O	O
B	G	P	M	K	C	O	A	S	T	E	N
I	R	I	O	E	F	G	M	Q	O	E	S
A	Y	Y	M	Y	X	M	A	P	Z	M	S
S	N	O	R	T	H	I	I	(B	A	Y)	P
U	D	R	I	V	E	R	C	L	F	S	G
N	E	A	S	T	E	R	N	O	E	W	S

Name _____

Activity 5   Finding My Way in the Western United States

Use Map 14. Circle the letter of the name or word that best answers each question.

1. In which state is San Diego located?
   a. Arizona   c. Utah
   b. California   d. Washington

2. In which state is Phoenix located?
   a. Arizona   c. Utah
   b. California   d. Washington

3. In which state is Salt Lake City located?
   a. Arizona   c. Utah
   b. California   d. Washington

4. In which state is Spokane located?
   a. Arizona   c. Utah
   b. California   d. Washington

5. Which city is located north of Eugene?
   a. Phoenix   c. San Francisco
   b. Salt Lake City   d. Portland

6. Which city is located east of San Diego?
   a. Phoenix   c. San Francisco
   b. Boise   d. Spokane

7. Which city is located northwest of San Diego?
   a. Phoenix   c. San Francisco
   b. Salt Lake City   d. Spokane

8. Which city is located north of Phoenix?
   a. Los Angeles   c. Salt Lake City
   b. Reno   d. Santa Fe

9. Which city is located northeast of Phoenix?
   a. Los Angeles   c. Salt Lake City
   b. Reno   d. Santa Fe

10. If you went east from Helena, which city would you reach?
    a. Billings   c. Eugene
    b. Boise   d. Salt Lake City

11. If you went southwest from Helena, which city would you reach?
    a. Billings   c. Boise
    b. Casper   d. Salt Lake City

12. In what direction is Spokane from Seattle?
    a. north   c. east
    b. south   d. west

13. In what direction is Boise from Denver?
    a. northwest   c. southwest
    b. northeast   d. southeast

14. In what direction is Eugene from Portland?
    a. north   c. east
    b. south   d. west

15. In what direction is Denver from Cheyenne?
    a. north   c. east
    b. south   d. west

Name _____

Activity 6 Understanding Orientation and Direction: A CROSSWORD PUZZLE

Use the clues on the next page to solve the puzzle below. Write one letter in each box.

The Language of Maps copyright © 1983 by Pitman Learning, Inc.

Name _____

Activity 6 (continued)

ACROSS

1. Midday
4. Opposite of *dusk*
8. Your image shown by the sun
13. Cry of pain
14. Section of a book
16. Northeast (abbreviation)
17. Music disc
21. When a fruit is ready to eat, it is _____ .
22. Mister (abbreviation)
23. Shouts from an audience wanting more
25. Leave out
28. I am, she is, you _____
29. Throw
31. You were, he _____
35. Magnetic arrow in a compass
38. It shines during the day.
39. While
41. Sheep's cry
43. Instrument that tells you directions
45. Flower
46. Enemy
48. Sphere or globe
49. Past tense of *sit*
50. Weight (abbreviation)
51. _____ Grande
52. Skim a page
54. Northwest (abbreviation)
55. Emotion
58. Connecticut (abbreviation)
59. Map symbol for a city
61. Purpose or goal
63. Symbol on a map
65. They make up the alphabet.
67. Rich soil
69. A sea or _____ ocean
70. Ship's distress signal
71. Grown males
72. Short, written composition

DOWN

1. Opposite of *south*
2. Be in debt
3. Kind of light used in store signs
5. Measure of land
6. Shrill sound
7. Short sleep
8. Street (abbreviation)
9. Border of a dress
10. Directional sign on map
11. Opposite of *off*
12. Opposite of *east*
15. _____ in a pod
18. Penny
19. Radio Corporation of America (abbreviation)
20. Girl's name
24. Note in musical scale
26. Drawings that represent parts of the earth's surface
27. Present tense of *was*
30. View
32. Northwest is an _____ direction.
33. North America (abbreviation)
34. Dot or line on a map
35. National Aeronautics and Space Administration (abbreviation)
36. Opposite of *west*
37. North, east, south, or west
40. Mark or grade
41. Sink or bowl-shaped depression in the earth
42. Map legend
44. A compass rose _____ the map for you.
47. Have
52. Shows distance in a map key
53. North and South _____
56. Freezes
57. Fuel
60. Note in musical scale
62. Massachusetts (abbreviation)
64. Negative vote
66. From here _____ there
68. Maine (abbreviation)

Symbolization

Name _____

Activity 7
Climbing My Way to the Top with Symbols and Landforms: A PUZZLE

The words listed on the next page are hidden below in the cross section of a sample landform structure of the earth. The words are arranged across (either left to right or right to left), down, up, and diagonally. Climb your way to the top by finding and circling each word in the cross section. Place a check next to each word in the list as you circle it in the cross section. The word PEAK has been done for you.

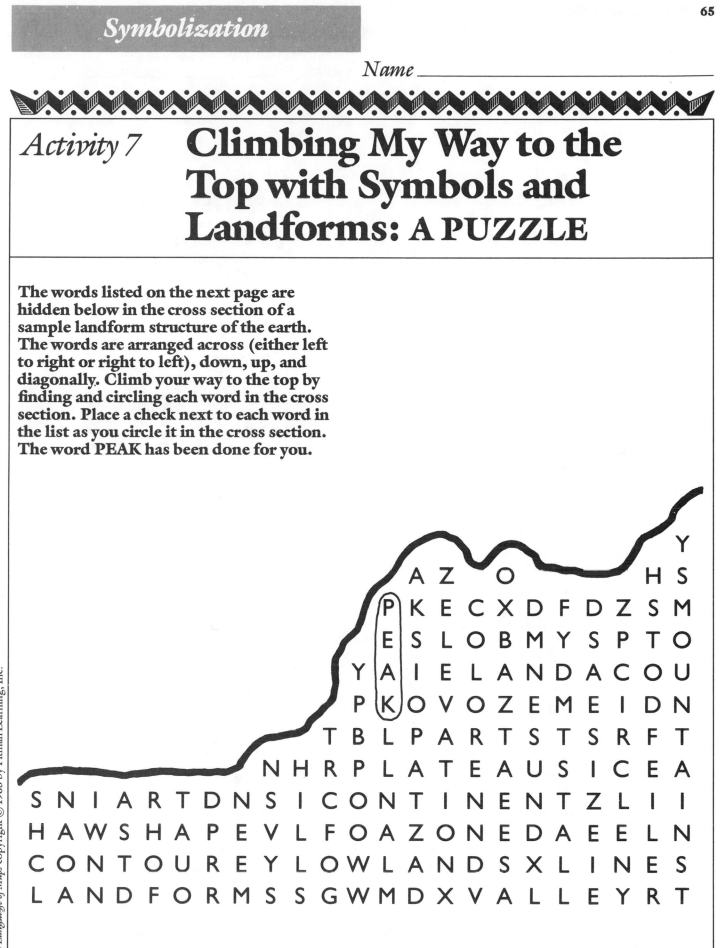

Name _____

AM	ORE
AN	PARTS
ARM	✓ PEAK
CIRCLE	PLAINS
COLD	RAINS
COLOR	RAN
CONTINENT	RELIEF
CONTOUR	RIVER
DOTS	SAND
ELEVATION	SAP
FOG	SEAS
HILLS	SHAPE
KEY	SIZE
LAND	SLOW
LANDFORMS	SO
LET	SOON
LIE	STALL
LINES	SUN
LOW	SYMBOLS
LOWLANDS	TEN
MAPS	UP
MOUNTAINS	VALLEY
MY	ZONED
ON	

Name _____

Activity 8   Comparing a Photo and a Map

Use Photo 1 and Map 1. Circle the letter of the word or phrase that best answers each question.

1. Which shows a key?
   a. photo   c. both
   b. map   d. neither

2. Which shows trees?
   a. photo   c. both
   b. map   d. neither

3. Which shows buildings?
   a. photo   c. both
   b. map   d. neither

4. Which shows grass?
   a. photo   c. both
   b. map   d. neither

5. Which shows a school?
   a. photo   c. both
   b. map   d. neither

6. Which shows cars?
   a. photo   c. both
   b. map   d. neither

7. Which shows streets?
   a. photo   c. both
   b. map   d. neither

8. Which shows directions or a directional sign?
   a. photo   c. both
   b. map   d. neither

9. Which shows more details or things?
   a. photo   c. both
   b. map   d. neither

10. Which shows the schoolyard in detail?
    a. photo   c. both
    b. map   d. neither

Name _____

Activity 9   Matching Elevation Symbols and Word Descriptions

A Cross Section of Land

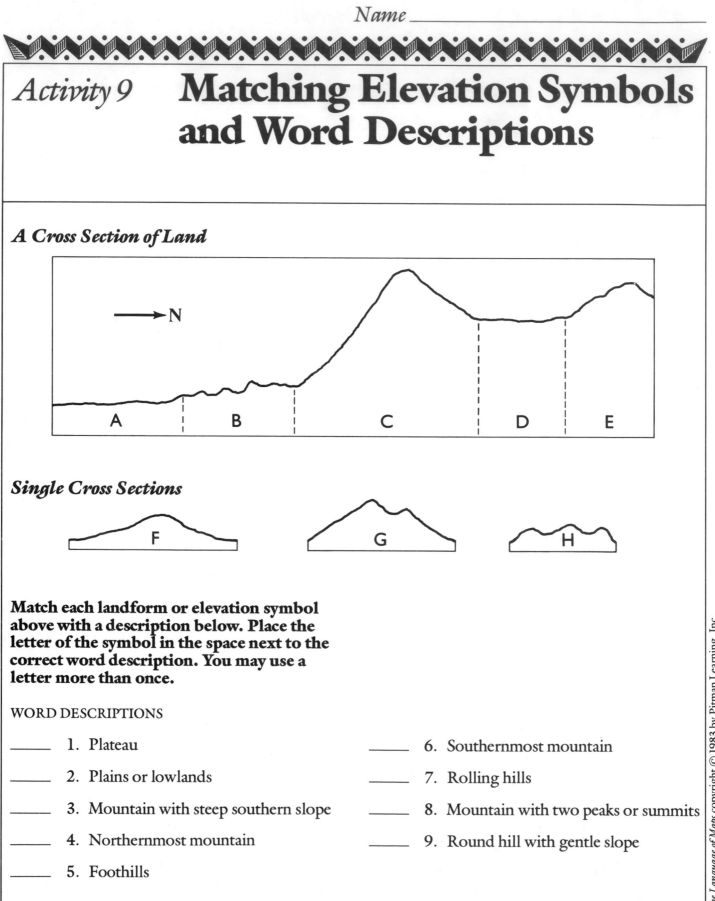

Single Cross Sections

Match each landform or elevation symbol above with a description below. Place the letter of the symbol in the space next to the correct word description. You may use a letter more than once.

WORD DESCRIPTIONS

_____ 1. Plateau

_____ 2. Plains or lowlands

_____ 3. Mountain with steep southern slope

_____ 4. Northernmost mountain

_____ 5. Foothills

_____ 6. Southernmost mountain

_____ 7. Rolling hills

_____ 8. Mountain with two peaks or summits

_____ 9. Round hill with gentle slope

Name _____

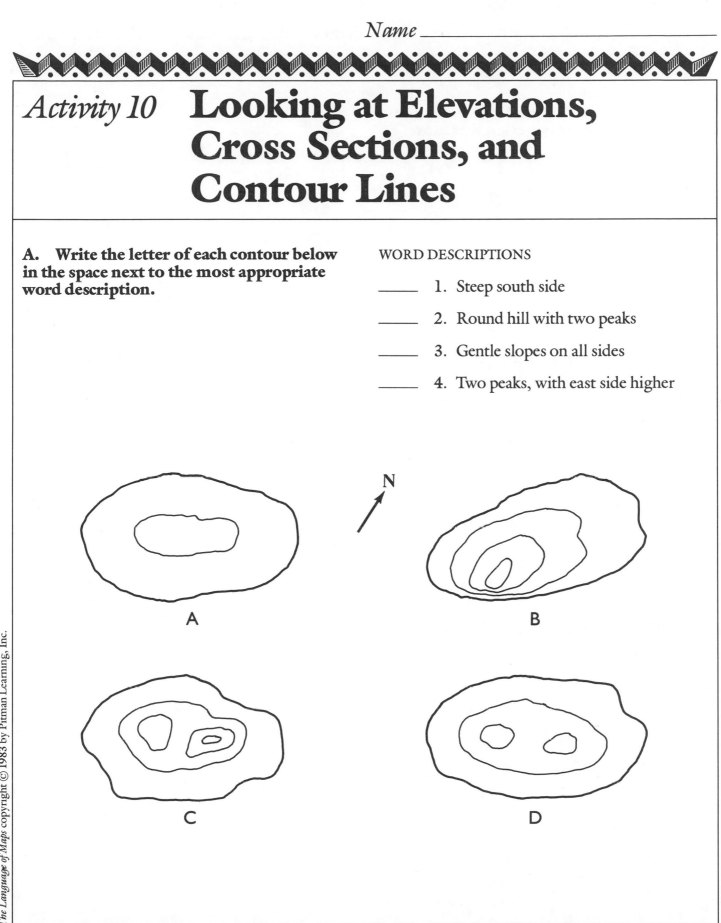

Activity 10 Looking at Elevations, Cross Sections, and Contour Lines

A.   Write the letter of each contour below in the space next to the most appropriate word description.

WORD DESCRIPTIONS

_____ 1. Steep south side

_____ 2. Round hill with two peaks

_____ 3. Gentle slopes on all sides

_____ 4. Two peaks, with east side higher

N

A

B

C

D

Name _____

Activity 10 (continued)

B.   Write the letter of each contour in the space next to the cross section that most closely matches it.

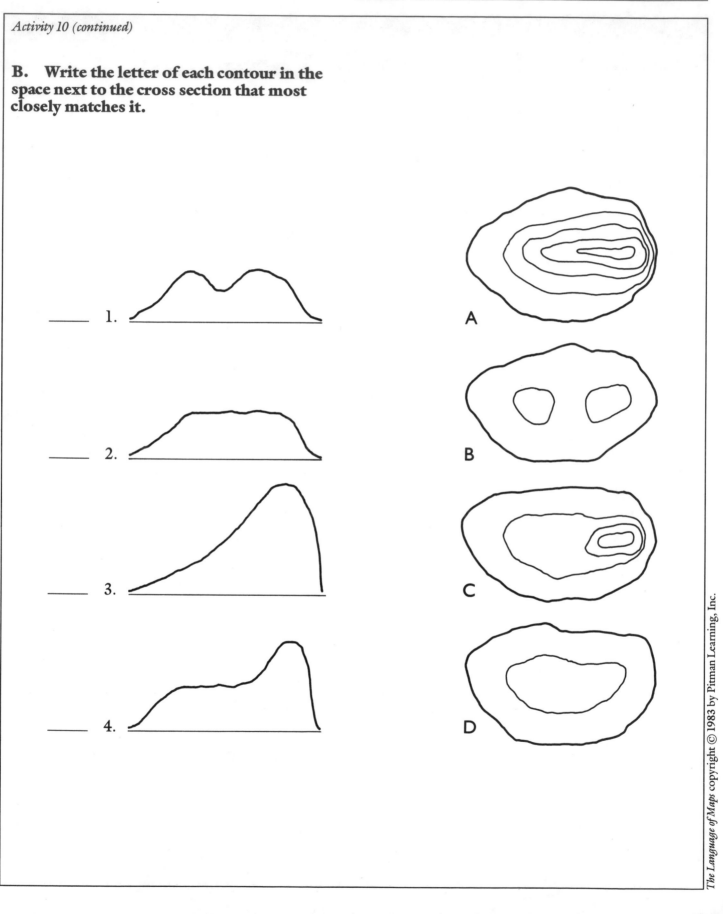

_____ 1.

_____ 2.

_____ 3.

_____ 4.

A

B

C

D

Name _____

Activity 11 **Using Map Terms:**
A PUZZLE

Use the words from the list on the next page to complete the criss-cross puzzle below. Place a check next to each term as you use it. SOUTH AMERICA has been filled in for you. Remember that some words go across and some words go down.

Name _____

AIR	IF	PLAINS
AM	IN	PLATEAUS
AN	IT	POST
AT	LANDFORMS	ROADS
CAT	LINE	ROLLING
CONTOUR	LO	SE
CREEK	LOT	SECTION
CUBA	LOW	SHAPE
DIAGRAM	LOWLAND	SIZE
DO	MAP	SO
DOT	MOUNTAINS	✓ SOUTH AMERICA
DOWN	NE	SPAIN
EACH	NOR	STEEP
FOR	NOT	STOP
GO	NW	STRAIT
HAITI	ONE	SUMMIT
HI	PEAKS	SW
HILLS	PHOTOS	UP
HOT	PHYSICAL	USE

Name _____

Activity 12 Comparing Countries and Landforms of South America

Use Map 2. Circle the letter of the word or phrase that best answers the question or best completes each sentence.

1. This is a map of what continent or landmass?
   a. North American   c. Africa
   b. South America   d. Asia

2. What kind of map is this?
   a. political   c. both
   b. physical   d. neither

3. Why is it the kind of map you named?
   a. shows boundary lines
   b. shows landform types
   c. shows boundaries and landforms
   d. none of the above

4. Where are most of the mountains located?
   a. west coast   c. inland
   b. east coast   d. south coast

5. Where are most of the plains located?
   a. west coast   c. inland
   b. east coast   d. south coast

6. Where is the largest plateau area located?
   a. west coast   c. inland
   b. east coast   d. south coast

7. Near what body of water are most of the mountains located?
   a. Caribbean Sea   c. Atlantic Ocean
   b. Pacific Ocean   d. none of the above

8. Chile is mostly _____ .
   a. mountains   c. hills
   b. plains   d. plateaus

9. Peru is mostly _____ .
   a. mountains   c. hills
   b. plains   d. plateaus

10. Ecuador is mostly _____ .
    a. mountains   c. hills
    b. plains   d. plateaus

11. Paraguay is mostly _____ .
    a. mountains   c. hills
    b. plains   d. plateaus

12. Uruguay is mostly _____ .
    a. mountains   c. hills
    b. plains   d. plateaus

13. Which country has the most plateau area?
    a. Argentina   c. Chile
    b. Brazil   d. Paraguay

14. Which country has the greatest area?
    a. Argentina   c. Chile
    b. Brazil   d. Paraguay

15. In what country is the Amazon River located?
    a. Suriname   c. Venezuela
    b. Argentina   d. Brazil

Name _____

Activity 13 Clarifying Geographic and Map Meanings

Circle the letter of the word or phrase that best completes the sentence or best answers the question.

1. To understand a map, you need to know that the legend means the _____ .
   a. key   c. story
   b. title   d. scale

2. To understand a map, you need to know that a dot, circle, or point is a symbol for _____ .
   a. a country   c. a town or city
   b. a road   d. the title

3. A line on a map may represent _____ .
   a. a river   c. a boundary
   b. a road   d. all of the above

4. Elevation may be shown with _____ .
   a. lines   c. shadings
   b. dots   d. all of the above

5. Contour lines on maps show _____ .
   a. roads   c. elevation
   b. highways   d. all of the above

6. A map is a selected _____ of the real thing.
   a. aerial view   c. both
   b. cross section   d. neither

7. A physical map shows _____ .
   a. elevation   c. both
   b. types of landforms d. neither

8. A physical map also may show _____ .
   a. cities   c. both
   b. rivers   d. neither

9. The scale in the key of a map indicates the _____ .
   a. legend   c. elevation
   b. distance   d. landmarks

10. A compass rose is used to show _____ on a map.
    a. roads   c. decorations
    b. directions d. continents

11. A _____ is a high, level land area within a mountain range.
    a. elevation   c. plateau
    b. lowland   d. plain

12. Which landform has the lowest elevation of all?
    a. mountains   c. hills
    b. plateaus   d. plains

13. Which best describes the slope of a mountain?
    a. the highest point
    b. the lowest point
    c. the side of a mountain
    d. the plateau

14. Which best describes the peak of a mountain?
    a. the highest point
    b. the plateau
    c. the side of a mountain
    d. the lowest point

15. An aerial view of a mountain can best be represented by using _____ .
    a. boundary lines   c. contour lines
    b. a cross-section   d. a compass rose
       drawing

Name _____

Activity 14 Matching Countries and Rivers of North America with Location and Size

Use Map 13. Circle the letter of the word or phrase that best answers each question.

1. Which country is the smallest in size?
   a. Canada   c. Mexico
   b. Cuba   d. United States

2. Which country is the largest in size?
   a. Canada   c. Mexico
   b. Cuba   d. United States

3. Which is an island country?
   a. Canada   c. Mexico
   b. Cuba   d. United States

4. Which river appears to be the longest?
   a. Colorado River
   b. Columbia River
   c. Mississippi River
   d. Rio Grande

5. Which river appears to be the shortest?
   a. Colorado River
   b. Missouri River
   c. Mississippi River
   d. Rio Grande

6. Which river does not end at a gulf?
   a. Colorado River
   b. Columbia River
   c. Mississippi River
   d. Rio Grande

7. Which nation is the smallest in size?
   a. Cuba   c. Nicaragua
   b. Dominican Republic   d. Jamaica

8. Which island nation is the largest in size?
   a. Cuba   c. Haiti
   b. Dominican Republic   d. Jamaica

9. Which two nations are not connected to each other by land?
   a. Cuba and Haiti
   b. Haiti and the Dominican Republic
   c. Canada and the United States
   d. Mexico and the United States

10. Which country seems to be larger from north to south than from east to west?
    a. Canada   c. Mexico
    b. Cuba   d. United States

11. Which river does not form or cross a border between two countries?
    a. Yukon River   c. Rio Grande
    b. Columbia River   d. Peace River

12. Which river ends at the Pacific Ocean?
    a. Yukon River   c. Mackenzie River
    b. Columbia River   d. Peace River

13. Which river does not end at an ocean or a sea?
    a. Yukon River   c. Mackenzie River
    b. Columbia River   d. Peace River

14. Which river does not connect with the Mississippi River?
    a. Rio Grande   c. Ohio River
    b. Red River   d. Arkansas River

15. On which country does Hudson Bay border?
    a. United States   c. Mexico
    b. Cuba   d. Canada

Name _____

Activity 15   **Recalling and Generalizing**

Circle the letter of the word or phrase that best completes the sentence or best answers the question.

1. Which is most likely to have the highest elevation?
   a. hills   c. plains
   b. mountains   d. plateaus

2. Which is most likely to have the lowest elevation?
   a. hills   c. plains
   b. mountains   d. plateaus

3. Which is usually at higher elevations than plateaus?
   a. hills   c. plains
   b. mountains   d. rivers

4. Which is more likely to be at lower elevations than hills?
   a. hills   c. plains
   b. mountains   d. plateaus

5. Which symbols are likely to be used to show elevation?
   a. color   c. neither
   b. lines   d. both

6. Contour lines are used to show an air view of _____ .
   a. cities   c. elevation
   b. oceans   d. population

7. A cross section is used to show a side view of _____ .
   a. elevation   c. continents
   b. color   d. population

8. A political map is used to show _____ .
   a. elevation   c. continents
   b. color   d. boundaries

9. A map that shows how high or low land and water are may be called a _____ .
   a. political map   c. neither
   b. population map   d. both

10. A map that shows the height and depth of land may be called a _____ .
    a. political map   c. neither
    b. physical map   d. both

Name _____

Activity 16 Interpreting Part of a Town Map

Use Map 15. Circle the letter of the numeral, letter, or phrase that best answers each question.

1. How many blocks is it from house C to the school?
   a. 3   c. 5
   b. 4   d. 6

2. Which house is nearest to the school?
   a. house A   c. house C
   b. house B   d. house D

3. From which street do people enter the church?
   a. Callings Street   c. Third Street
   b. Dawn Street   d. Church Street

4. Which street ends at the park?
   a. Second Street   c. Baker Street
   b. Third Street   d. Callings Street

5. Which street is two blocks north of Fairview Street?
   a. Baker Street   c. Dawn Street
   b. Callings Street   d. Everett Street

6. How many blocks is it from house A to house B?
   a. 2   c. 5
   b. 3   d. 6

7. If Pat leaves house G and goes north along Third Street, in which direction and on which street would she have to turn to get to school?
   a. right onto Callings Street
   b. left onto Callings Street
   c. left onto Baker Street
   d. right onto Alpine Street

8. John lives in house H, on Goshin Street between Third and Fourth streets. Which is another way to say where John lives?
   a. three blocks from house C
   b. across from the church
   c. across from house G
   d. four blocks from the school

9. Jane lives in house C. When she goes to school, she passes by the church, which is on the corner of which streets?
   a. Second and Callings streets
   b. Third and Callings streets
   c. Fourth and Callings streets
   d. Fourth and Dawn streets

10. Joel lives in house F. When he goes to school by way of Fifth Street, he passes by the synagogue, which is between which streets?
   a. Everett and Fifth streets
   b. Dawn and Everett streets
   c. Fourth and Everett streets
   d. Fifth and Callings streets

Name _____

The Language of Maps copyright © 1983 by Pitman Learning, Inc.

Activity 16 (continued)

11. Going to school along Fifth Street, where and in which direction would Joel have to turn to get to school?
    a. right onto Callings Street
    b. left onto Callings Street
    c. left onto Baker Street
    d. right onto Baker Street

12. Who lives closest to the synagogue?
    a. Adeline from house E
    b. Joel from house F
    c. Pat from house G
    d. John from house H

13. Who lives farthest from the synagogue?
    a. Adeline from house E
    b. Joel from house F
    c. Pat from house G
    d. Karen from house D

14. Which house is located farthest east?
    a. house A   c. house E
    b. house C   d. house H

15. Which house is located farthest south?
    a. house A   c. house E
    b. house C   d. house H

Name _____

Activity 17 **Recognizing Word Relationships: ANTONYMS**

An *antonym* is a word that means the opposite of another word; for example, *bad* is an antonym for *good*. Circle the letter of the word or phrase that best completes each sentence.

1. East is to west as northward is to _____ .
   a. westward c. southward
   b. pole   d. south

2. Uphill is to downhill as south is to _____ .
   a. mouth c. north
   b. month d. fourth

3. Close is to far as nearest is to _____ .
   a. farthest c. closest
   b. fattest d. longest

4. Shortest is to longest as lowest is to _____ .
   a. farthest c. closest
   b. fattest d. highest

5. Near is to distant as close is to _____ .
   a. home c. bar
   b. far d. shut

6. Hill is to dale as mountain is to _____ .
   a. plateau c. elevation
   b. valley d. sail

7. Mountains are to plateaus as hills are to _____ .
   a. highlands c. depressions
   b. lowlands d. elevations

8. Steep is to gentle as deep is to _____ .
   a. rental c. shallow
   b. heap d. fallow

9. Bottom is to top as sea level is to _____ .
   a. mountain peak c. stop
   b. plain   d. hill

10. Inland is to coastal as eastern is to _____ .
    a. northern c. western
    b. southern d. postal

Name _____

Activity 18   Interpreting a Road Map of Part of the Great Lakes Area

Use Map 16. Circle the letter of the word or phrase that best answers each question.

1. If you were going from Watertown to Syracuse, which highway would you take?
   a. U.S. Highway 75
   b. U.S. Highway 81
   c. U.S. Highway 90
   d. New York Highway 18

2. If you returned to Watertown from Syracuse, in what general direction would you be going?
   a. north   c. east
   b. south   d. west

3. With which two highways does U.S. Highway 81 connect?
   a. U.S. Highway 90 and New York Highway 18
   b. U.S. Highway 90 and Canada Highway 401
   c. Canada Highway 401 and New York Highway 18
   d. Canada Highway 90 and U.S. Highway 401

4. If you went from Detroit to Windsor, which city could you get to by continuing along Canada Highway 401?
   a. Brantford   c. London
   b. Hamilton   d. Flint

5. If you went from Rochester to Hamilton along New York Highway 18, which other highway must you take?
   a. Canada Highway 20
   b. Canada Highway 24
   c. Canada Highway 401
   d. Canada Highway 402

6. Which highway is the route from Brantford to Cambridge?
   a. Canada Highway 2
   b. Canada Highway 24
   c. Canada Highway 20
   d. Canada Highway 401

7. Which city is not located on or near U.S. Highway 90?
   a. Buffalo   c. Erie
   b. Detroit   d. Syracuse

8. Which city is not located on or near Canada Highway 401?
   a. Cambridge   c. Oshawa
   b. Hamilton   d. Toronto

9. Which city is not located on or near U.S. Highway 75?
   a. Bay City   c. Brantford
   b. Detroit   d. Flint

Name _____

Activity 18 (continued)

10. In what general direction would you travel to get from London to Hamilton?
    a. north   c. east
    b. south   d. west

11. Which city is located along Lake Erie?
    a. Brantford   c. Buffalo
    b. Hamilton   d. Port Huron

12. Which city is located along Lake Ontario?
    a. Brantford   c. Buffalo
    b. Hamilton   d. Port Huron

13. To go from Kingston to Watertown along highways 401 and 81, how must you travel?
    a. south over the St. Lawrence River
    b. north over the St. Lawrence River
    c. south over Lake Ontario
    d. north over Lake Ontario

14. Which city is nearest to Toronto by highway?
    a. Oshawa   c. Detroit
    b. Buffalo   d. London

15. Which city is farthest from Toronto by highway?
    a. Oshawa   c. Detroit
    b. Buffalo   d. London

Name _____

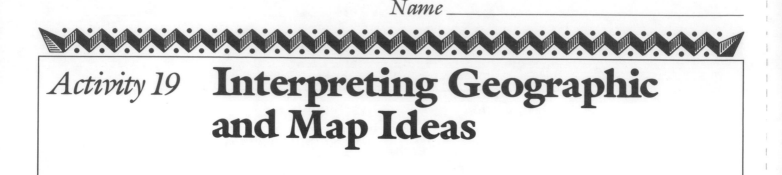

Activity 19 Interpreting Geographic and Map Ideas

Circle the letter of the word or phrase that best completes the sentence or best answers the question.

1. To know what a map shows, the first thing you need to do is read the _____ .
   a. compass rose   c. key
   b. title   d. date

2. To know whether or not a map is a current one, you need to know the _____ .
   a. compass rose
   b. title
   c. key
   d. date of publication

3. Before you can interpret the symbols on a map, you need to find _____ .
   a. the key
   b. the symbols on the map
   c. the scale
   d. the directions

4. To determine in which direction to go on a map, you first need to _____ .
   a. orient yourself
   b. find the scale
   c. find the beginning location
   d. find your destination

5. Once you know the symbols for the starting and stopping places and you know the directions, you need to _____ .
   a. orient yourself to the map
   b. find the scale in the key
   c. find the beginning and ending locations
   d. find the title of the map

6. Once you know where you are and where you are going, you need to _____ .
   a. determine the distance using the scale
   b. find the beginning and ending locations
   c. find the scale
   d. find and trace the route to your destination

7. Once you know how you will reach your destination, to find out how far it is you must _____ .
   a. find your compass
   b. find the beginning and ending locations
   c. find the scale
   d. find and trace the route to your destination

8. What do you do next to find out how far away your destination is?
   a. Determine the distance using the scale.
   b. Find the beginning and ending locations.
   c. Find the scale.
   d. Find and trace the route to your destination.

9. If you want to know where the gas stations and restaurants are along the way, where on the map must you look first?
   a. the compass rose   c. the route
   b. the key   d. the scale

10. Once you have found the symbols for gas stations and restaurants, where on the map do you look next?
   a. the compass rose   c. the route
   b. the key   d. the scale

Activity 20 **Reading Road Signs**

Imagine that you are standing in front of the four road signs below. Circle the letter of the place or road sign that best answers each question on the next page.

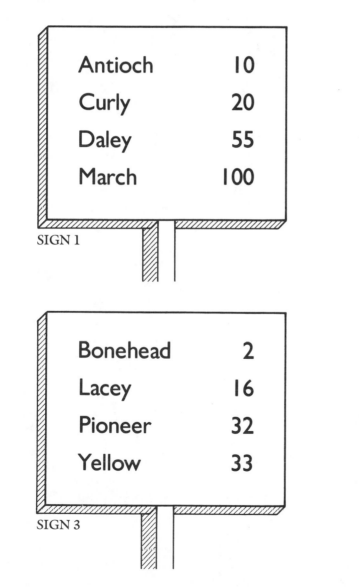

Antioch	10
Curly	20
Daley	55
March	100

SIGN 1

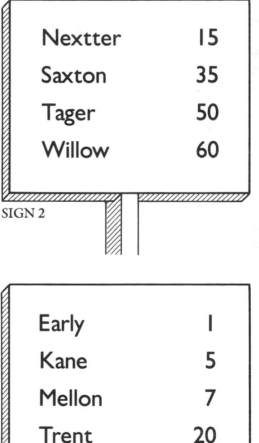

Nextter	15
Saxton	35
Tager	50
Willow	60

SIGN 2

Bonehead	2
Lacey	16
Pioneer	32
Yellow	33

SIGN 3

Early	1
Kane	5
Mellon	7
Trent	20

SIGN 4

Activity 20 (continued)

1. Which road sign would you follow to go to Trent?
   a. 1   c. 3
   b. 2   d. 4

2. Which road sign indicates the nearest city or town?
   a. 1   c. 3
   b. 2   d. 4

3. Which road sign indicates the farthest city or town?
   a. 1   c. 3
   b. 2   d. 4

4. According to sign 1, which city is halfway between Antioch and March?
   a. Lacey   c. Curly
   b. Daley   d. none of the above

5. According to sign 2, to which city is Saxton closest?
   a. Nextter   c. Tager
   b. Daley   d. Willow

6. According to sign 1, which city is 10 times as far away as Antioch?
   a. Trent   c. March
   b. Curly   d. Willow

7. If you were going to Pioneer by way of Bonehead, which road sign would you follow?
   a. 1   c. 3
   b. 2   d. 4

8. If you were going to Willow by way of Nextter, which road sign would you follow?
   a. 1   c. 3
   b. 2   d. 4

9. If you were going to Kane, which road sign would you follow?
   a. 1   c. 3
   b. 2   d. 4

10. Which city is only one mile away?
    a. Early   c. Yellow
    b. Pioneer   d. Bonehead

Name _____

Activity 21   Using Road Signs in Reading a Road Map

Use Map 11. Circle the letter of the word or phrase that best answers each question.

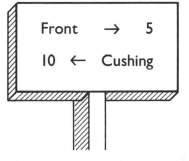

Front   →   5

10   ←   Cushing

1. The towns of Ash and Box are located on which highway?
   a. U.S. Highway 16
   b. U.S. Highway 32
   c. State Highway 7
   d. State Highway 9

2. How far is it from Cushing to Delta?
   a. 6 miles   c. 15 miles
   b. 10 miles   d. 16 miles

3. In which direction would you travel to go from Delta to Helen?
   a. east   c. north
   b. west   d. south

4. Which U.S. highway ends at Helen?
   a. U.S. Highway 4
   b. U.S. Highway 16
   c. U.S. Highway 32
   d. U.S. Highway 67

5. Which town is farthest from Cushing?
   a. Ash   c. Delta
   b. Box   d. Eli

6. What kind of road connects Delta with U.S. Highway 16?
   a. graveled state highway
   b. paved state highway
   c. graveled U.S. highway
   d. paved U.S. highway

7. In which town would this sign be located?
   a. Box   c. Eli
   b. Delta   d. Helen

8. If you saw the sign in question 7 while you were traveling, in which direction would you be facing?
   a. north   c. east
   b. south   d. west

9. What are Front and Cushing?
   a. cities   c. a town and a city
   b. towns   d. a city and a town

10. Between which towns would you cross a bridge on State Highway 9?
    a. Ash and Box
    b. Ash and Cushing
    c. Cushing and Delta
    d. Delta and Helen

11. What kinds of roads have bridges crossing the river?
    a. paved state highways
    b. graveled and paved state highways
    c. paved U.S. highways
    d. U.S. and state highways

Name _____

Activity 21 (continued)

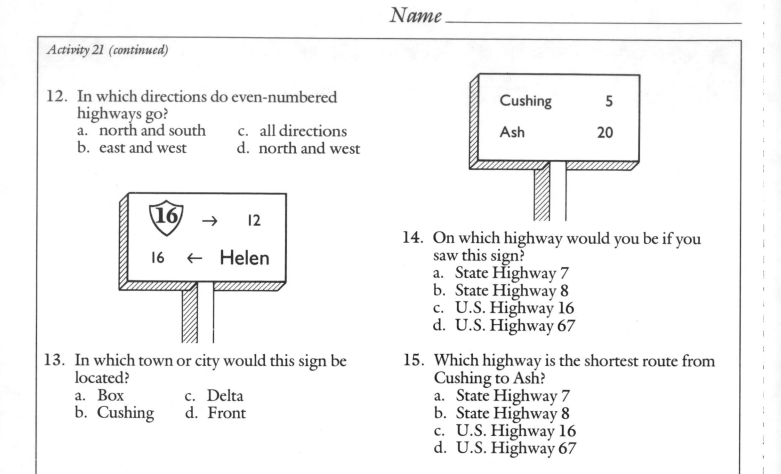

12. In which directions do even-numbered highways go?
   a. north and south
   b. east and west
   c. all directions
   d. north and west

13. In which town or city would this sign be located?
   a. Box
   b. Cushing
   c. Delta
   d. Front

14. On which highway would you be if you saw this sign?
   a. State Highway 7
   b. State Highway 8
   c. U.S. Highway 16
   d. U.S. Highway 67

15. Which highway is the shortest route from Cushing to Ash?
   a. State Highway 7
   b. State Highway 8
   c. U.S. Highway 16
   d. U.S. Highway 67

Name _____

Activity 22 Drawing Conclusions from Two Maps

Use Maps 2 and 17. Circle the letter of the word or phrase that best answers the question or best completes the sentence.

1. Where are most South American cities located?
   a. inland   c. plateaus
   b. near the coast d. hills

2. The two capital cities of Bolivia are located in the _____ .
   a. mountains c. hills
   b. plateaus   d. lowlands

3. In which country is Brasilia located?
   a. Argentina c. Brazil
   b. Bolivia   d. Paraguay

4. Which country does not have an inland city identified on the map?
   a. Argentina c. Colombia
   b. Chile   d. Venezuela

5. Where are the major Argentine cities located?
   a. mountains c. hills
   b. plateaus   d. plains

6. Where are most of the major Brazilian cities located?
   a. highlands
   b. inland plateaus
   c. coastal plains
   d. coastal mountains

7. How many cities are identified along or near the Amazon River?
   a. 1   c. 3
   b. 2   d. none

8. Most of the major cities along the west coast of South America are located in the _____ .
   a. mountains c. hills
   b. plateaus   d. lowlands

9. Most of the major cities along the east coast of South America are located in the _____ .
   a. mountains c. hills
   b. plateaus   d. lowlands

10. Which city is a plateau city?
    a. Asuncion c. Cuzco
    b. Brasilia d. Bogota

Name _____

Activity 23   Finding Capitals and Countries of South America: A WORD PUZZLE

A.   Use Map 17. Fill in the blanks with letters to spell the names of South American capital cities. One letter is given for each city to help you.

1.   __ __ __ __ **C** __ __ __

2.   __ __ __ **A** __ __ __

3.   __ **P** __ __ __ __ __ __ __ __

4.   __ **I** __

5.   __ __ __ __ **T** __

6.   __ __ **A** __ __ __ __ __

7.   __ **L** __   __ __ __

8.   __ __ __ **C** __ __ __

9.   __ __ **I** __ __

10.   __ __ __ __ __ **T** __ __

11.   __ __ __ __ **I** __ __

12.   __ __ __ **E** __

13.   __ __ __ __ __ **S** __ __ __ __ __

Name _____

Activity 23 (continued)

B.   Use Maps 2 and 17. Find out in which country each capital city you named in part A is located. Write the name of the country next to the number that matches the number of its capital city. Then answer the questions below.

1. _____   8. _____

2. _____   9. _____

3. _____   10. _____

4. _____   11. _____

5. _____   12. _____

6. _____   13. _____

7. _____

14. Which country is listed twice? _____

    Why? _____

    _____

15. Which country's capital is not listed in part A?

    _____

Name _____

Activity 24   **Reading a Story and a Photo Together**

Use Photo 4. Read the story below. Then circle the letter of the word or phrase that best answers the question or best completes the sentence.

STORY

Photo 4 is an aerial view of part of California, photographed from a U-2 airplane. The San Francisco Bay Area is in the foreground. The snowcapped mountains in the background are called the Sierra Nevada.

In the left center of the photo, a portion of the Pacific Ocean (1) forms an inlet called the Golden Gate Straits (2). As you pass under the Golden Gate Bridge (it appears in the photo as a line joining the two land masses in the straits), you enter San Francisco Bay (3). Treasure Island (4) is in front of you and San Francisco (5) is to your right.

You stop at one of San Francisco's piers and go ashore. Notice that San Francisco is a *peninsula,* or land with water on three sides. To get across the bay you board a bus and go over the San Francisco–Oakland Bay Bridge (6). On the left, or northwest, side of the bridge is Treasure Island. When you reach the other side you find Berkeley to your left and Oakland to your right.

Your bus driver goes to the left, or north, on the freeway (7). He then turns left at Richmond (8) and goes toward the Richmond–San Rafael Bridge (9). When your bus crosses the bridge, your bus driver turns left again, this time southeast, onto the freeway (10) heading toward San Francisco. Along the way, he stops in the

Tiburon-Belvedere area (11) so that you can take a ferry boat to Angel Island (12). After you return to the bus, the driver goes back to the freeway and turns toward San Francisco. Soon you will cross the Golden Gate Bridge, bringing you back to San Francisco.

1. This is a photograph of _____ .
   a. Montreal
   b. Los Angeles
   c. the San Francisco Bay Area
   d. Mexico City

2. The photo's lower right-hand portion shows a great deal of _____ .
   a. forest   c. highways
   b. water   d. land

3. From the photo, most of the populated areas seem to be located near the _____ .
   a. water   c. mountains
   b. Angel Island   d. Treasure Island

4. Which number on the photo identifies the San Francisco–Oakland Bay Bridge?
   a. 1   c. 6
   b. 3   d. 7

5. Which number on the photo identifies the freeway in Berkeley?
   a. 7   c. 10
   b. 8   d. 12

Name _____

6. When you are going from Berkeley to Richmond along the freeway, you are going _____ .
   a. northeast   c. southwest
   b. northwest   d. southeast

7. Which bridge must you cross to go from Richmond to San Rafael?
   a. Golden Gate Bridge
   b. San Francisco – Oakland Bay Bridge
   c. Richmond – San Rafael Bridge
   d. none of the above

8. After going over the bridge to San Rafael, which direction did the driver turn?
   a. right   c. both
   b. southeast   d. neither

9. As the driver left the freeway to go to the Tiburon-Belvedere area, he turned _____ .
   a. right   c. south
   b. left   d. north

10. Where did you go when the driver stopped?
    a. Treasure Island   c. Angel Island
    b. Yerba Buena Island   d. San Rafael

11. Where is the island located?
    a. San Francisco Bay   c. both
    b. 3   d. neither

12. How did you get there?
    a. bus   c. airplane
    b. ship   d. ferry boat

13. Which bridge must you cross to reach San Francisco from the freeway that is to the northwest?
    a. Golden Gate Bridge
    b. San Francisco – Oakland Bay Bridge
    c. Richmond – San Rafael Bridge
    d. none of the above

14. The story ended by your bus driver taking you to _____ .
    a. San Rafael   c. San Francisco
    b. Angel Island   d. Oakland

15. San Francisco's main transportation connection with the communities across the bay is by means of _____ .
    a. airplanes   c. ships
    b. ferry boats   d. bridges

Name _____

Activity 25　**Drawing Conclusions from a Story and a Map**

Use Map 13. Read the story below. Then circle the letter of the word or phrase that best answers each question.

STORY

Evan lived in Toronto. He was going to Acapulco for a winter holiday. His airline was to make a two-hour stop at Chicago, just **428** miles away, on the way to Acapulco. Evan planned to take a taxi tour of Chicago during the stopover.

Evan boarded the plane, and it took off at the scheduled time. All went well until just before the plane was to land. The pilot reported that there was a snowstorm in Chicago. They would continue on to Kansas City, where landing would be safer.

The pilot said this change would make some problems. There were no direct flights from Kansas City to Acapulco. Passengers would have to fly from Kansas City to San Francisco and then go on to Acapulco. The next flight to San Francisco was not scheduled to leave Kansas City until the next morning. The airline would take the passengers to a hotel in Kansas City and return them to the airport for the morning flight. In San Francisco, the passengers would take another flight to Acapulco. The pilot made everybody feel better by reporting that the temperature in Acapulco was **94** degrees.

Evan sat back, disappointed and a little confused by all these changes. He was glad for one thing, though. He had planned to spend his winter holiday in Acapulco, not Chicago! He put his head back and went to sleep with a smile on his face.

1. Which statement best describes Evan?
   a. He lives in Canada and is going to Cuba.
   b. He lives in the United States and is going to Canada.
   c. He lives in Canada and is going to California.
   d. He lives in Canada and is going to Mexico.

2. To which city is Evan going on a vacation?
   a. Chicago　　c. San Francisco
   b. Acapulco　　d. Kansas City

3. Where is Evan's winter holiday destination located?
   a. west coast　　c. inland
   b. east coast　　d. Atlantic seaboard

4. Why was his plane flying to Kansas City instead of Chicago?
   a. because it was hijacked
   b. because of bad weather
   c. so he could sleep overnight
   d. to take him to San Francisco

5. When Evan left Toronto, his plane was headed southwest to Chicago. To reach Kansas City, in which direction would the plane need to go?
   a. southeast　　c. west
   b. southwest　　d. south

Name _____

6. Why would the next flight take him from Kansas City to San Francisco and not directly to his destination?
   a. **There was no direct flight from Kansas City to his destination.**
   b. Evan wanted to see part of San Francisco.
   c. Evan wanted to visit another city.
   d. Evan wanted another stop.

7. From Kansas City, in which direction would Evan's jet fly the next day?
   a. southeast   c. west
   b. southwest   d. south

8. To reach his destination from San Francisco, in which direction would Evan's flight go?
   a. southeast   c. west
   b. southwest   d. south

9. Which city in Evan's trip is located along or near the Great Lakes?
   a. Chicago   c. San Francisco
   b. Kansas City   d. Acapulco

10. Along which coast is San Francisco located?
    a. west coast   c. both
    b. Pacific coast   d. neither

11. Which city is not an inland city?
    a. Toronto   c. San Francisco
    b. Chicago   d. Kansas City

12. Which west coast city was having warm winter weather?
    a. San Francisco   c. both
    b. Acapulco   d. neither

13. Which river might the San Francisco–Acapulco flight cross?
    a. Mississippi River
    b. Missouri River
    c. Columbia River
    d. Colorado River

14. Why was Evan glad that he was going to spend his holiday in Acapulco and not in Chicago?
    a. It was too hot in Chicago.
    b. He couldn't stop in Chicago.
    c. It was warm in Acapulco.
    d. It was on the west coast.

15. When the story ended, where was Evan?
    a. landing in Acapulco
    b. on the flight to San Francisco
    c. in a Kansas City hotel
    d. in the plane near Chicago

PART III

Answer Key

Activity 1

```
I N   Y A R D S T I C K
I N O   F   U   T O
D I R E C T I O N   M Y
O   T   E     G A P
O H O U R   W A ▮ A M
R N   N E E D L E S
  M   O ▮ S ▮ E ▮ S
S A   S O U T H   P   M
H U G E ▮ N   E O   A
A N F   M O R N I N G
D E R   R   E   N ▮ N
O U T D O O R     T I E
W I   M ▮ I       T
S C   E A S T   S O S
```

Activity 2

1. b	6. b	11. a
2. a	7. c	12. d
3. a	8. c	13. d
4. d	9. b	14. c
5. c	10. c	15. c

Activity 3

1. a	6. c	11. b
2. b	7. b	12. a
3. a	8. d	13. b
4. a	9. a	14. d
5. a	10. d	15. a

Activity 4

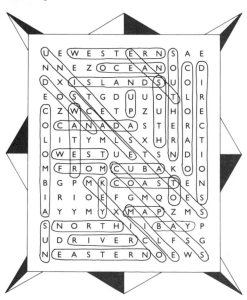

Activity 5

1. b	6. a	11. c
2. a	7. c	12. c
3. c	8. c	13. a
4. d	9. d	14. b
5. d	10. a	15. b

Activity 6

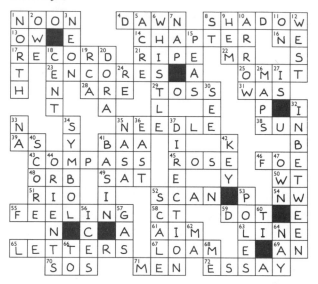

Activity 7

Activity 8

1. b	6. a
2. c	7. c
3. c	8. d
4. c	9. a
5. d	10. d

Activity 9

1. D	6. C
2. A	7. H
3. C	8. G
4. E	9. F
5. B	

Activity 10

A.		**B.**	
1. B		1. B	
2. D		2. D	
3. A		3. A	
4. C		4. C	

Activity 11

```
L O W   P H Y S I C A L     M A P
I N     L     O ■ R O T   O ■ E A C H
N E     A T   U S E T   C U B A   O N
E   D O T   S T E E P ■ S ■ N   K   N W
  O ■ E     H K   P H O T O S   T
L O W L A N D       A ■ A     F O R
A   N   U   A S   S P A I N     U R
N     S U M M I T   E   N O R     R
D O   H   P   E ■ R     S T O P   P
F O   A   R O A D S     L O   L A
O R   A I R   H I ■ I I   H I L L S   A
R     T     C A T   Z   O     I T   I
M   D I A G R A M   S E C T I O N   A N S
S O         O     W       F   G       S
```

Activity 12

1. b	6. c	11. b
2. c	7. b	12. b
3. c	8. a	13. b
4. a	9. a	14. b
5. c	10. a	15. d

Activity 13

1. a	6. a	11. c
2. c	7. c	12. d
3. d	8. b	13. c
4. d	9. b	14. a
5. c	10. b	15. c

Activity 14

1. b	6. b	11. d
2. a	7. d	12. b
3. b	8. a	13. d
4. c	9. a	14. a
5. a	10. c	15. d

Activity 15

1. b	6. c
2. c	7. a
3. b	8. d
4. c	9. c
5. d	10. b

Activity 16

1. a	6. b	11. b
2. d	7. a	12. b
3. c	8. c	13. c
4. a	9. b	14. c
5. c	10. b	15. d

Activity 17

1. c	6. b
2. c	7. b
3. a	8. c
4. d	9. a
5. b	10. c

Activity 18

1. b	6. b	11. c
2. a	7. b	12. b
3. b	8. b	13. a
4. c	9. c	14. a
5. a	10. c	15. c

Activity 19

1. b	6. d
2. d	7. c
3. a	8. a
4. a	9. b
5. c	10. c

Activity 20

1. d	6. c
2. d	7. c
3. a	8. b
4. b	9. d
5. c	10. a

Activity 21

1.	a	6.	a	11.	a
2.	c	7.	c	12.	b
3.	d	8.	c	13.	c
4.	c	9.	a	14.	d
5.	b	10.	d	15.	a

Activity 22

1.	b	6.	c
2.	a	7.	d
3.	c	8.	c
4.	d	9.	d
5.	d	10.	b

Activity 23

A.

1.	Asuncion	8.	Sucre
2.	Caracas	9.	Quito
3.	Paramaribo	10.	Georgetown
4.	Lima	11.	Santiago
5.	Bogota	12.	Montevideo
6.	Brasilia	13.	Buenos Aires
7.	La Paz		

B.

1. Paraguay
2. Venezuela
3. Suriname
4. Peru
5. Colombia
6. Brazil
7. Bolivia
8. Bolivia
9. Ecuador
10. Guyana
11. Chile
12. Uruguay
13. Argentina
14. Bolivia; because it has two capitals. (La Paz is used as the capital, although Sucre is the official capital.)
15. French Guiana

Activity 24

1.	c	6.	b	11.	c
2.	d	7.	c	12.	d
3.	a	8.	b	13.	a
4.	c	9.	b	14.	c
5.	a	10.	c	15.	d

Activity 25

1.	d	6.	a	11.	c
2.	b	7.	c	12.	b
3.	a	8.	a	13.	d
4.	b	9.	a	14.	c
5.	b	10.	c	15.	d

PART IV

Visuals

PHOTO I

PHOTO 2

PHOTO 3

The Language of Maps copyright © 1983 by David S. Lake Publishers.

PHOTO 4

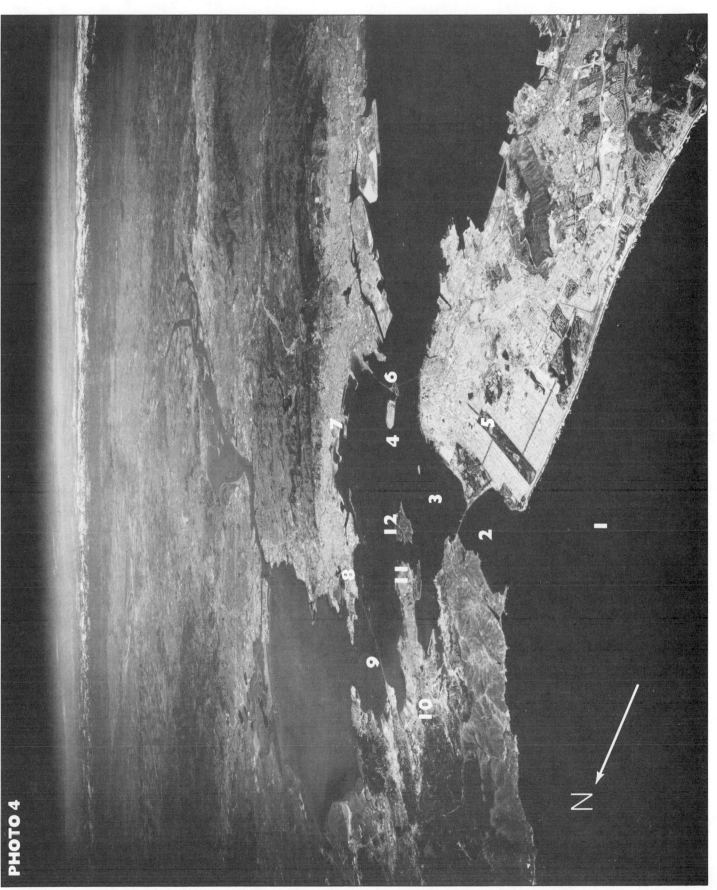

MAP I

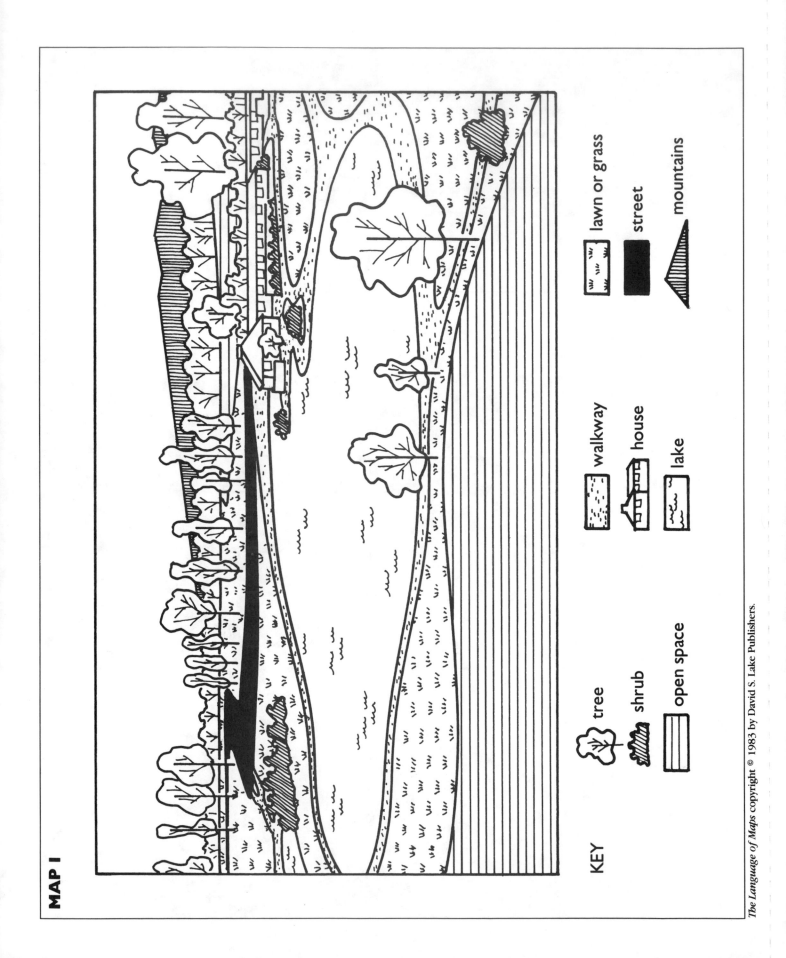

KEY

tree	walkway
shrub	house
open space	lake
	lawn or grass
	street
	mountains

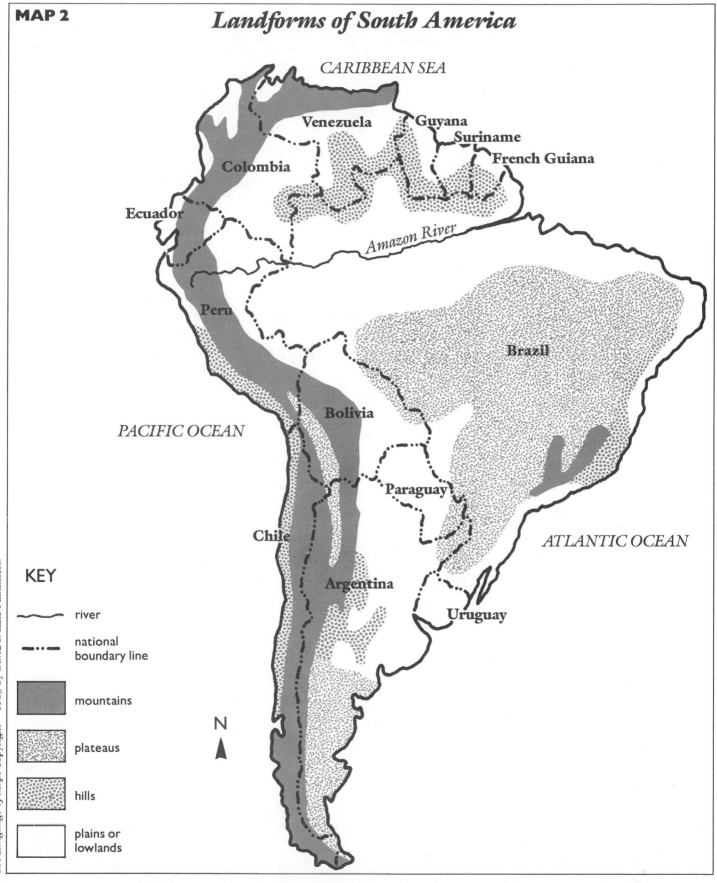

MAP 2

Landforms of South America

CARIBBEAN SEA

Venezuela
Guyana
Suriname
French Guiana

Colombia

Ecuador

Amazon River

Peru

Brazil

PACIFIC OCEAN

Bolivia

Paraguay

Chile

ATLANTIC OCEAN

Argentina

Uruguay

N

KEY

— river

—·—·— national
boundary line

mountains

plateaus

hills

plains or
lowlands

MAP 3

The United States in 1789

MAP 4

The United States in 1825

1789

1825

MAP 5

The United States in 1849

MAP 6

Populations of Canadian Cities

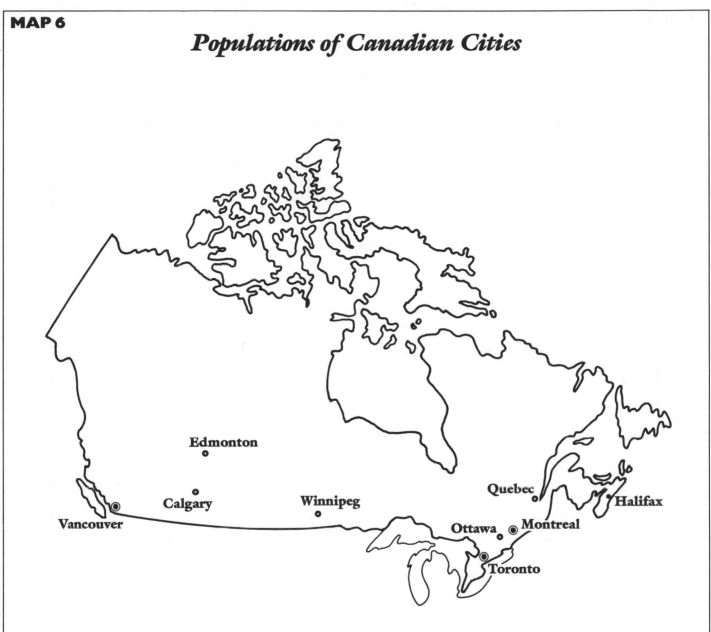

Edmonton

Calgary   Winnipeg

Vancouver

Quebec   Halifax

Ottawa   Montreal

Toronto

KEY

⊚ more than 1,000,000

⊙ between 500,000 and 1,000,000

• less than 500,000

MAP 7

Floor Plan of a Classroom

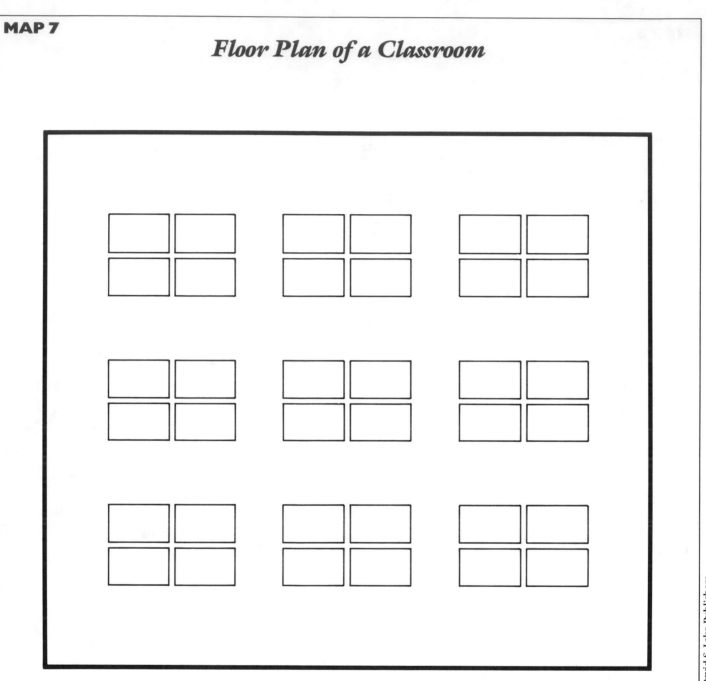

KEY

table or desk

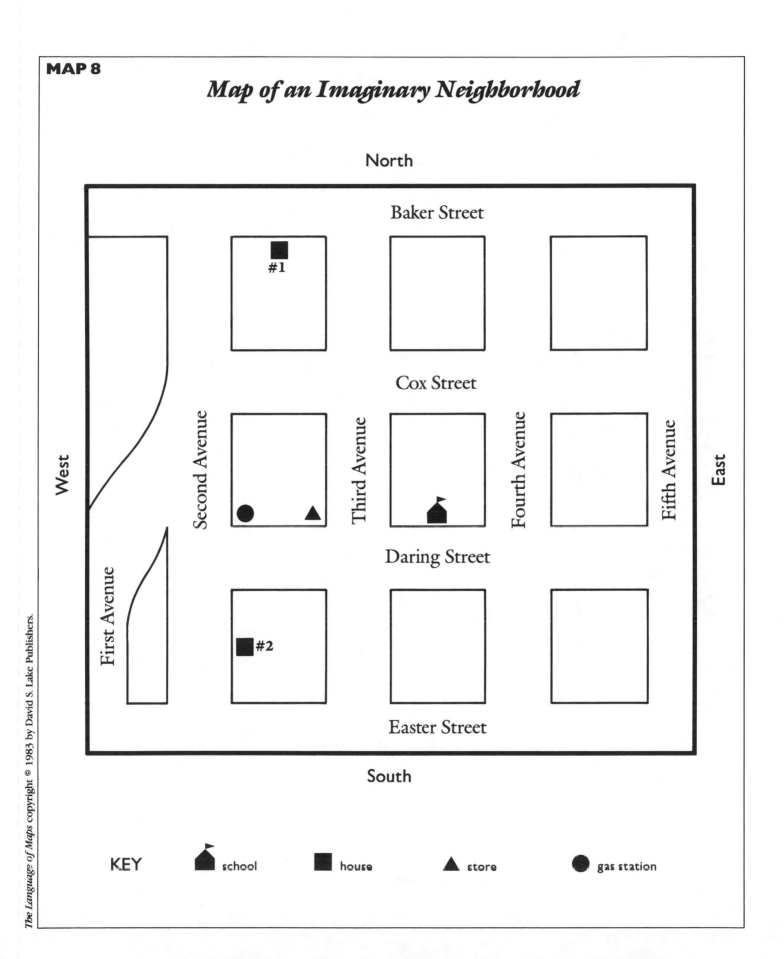

MAP 8

Map of an Imaginary Neighborhood

North

Baker Street

#1

Cox Street

West · Second Avenue · Third Avenue · Fourth Avenue · Fifth Avenue · East

First Avenue

Daring Street

#2

Easter Street

South

KEY   school   house   store   gas station

The Language of Maps copyright © 1983 by David S. Lake Publishers.

MAP 9

Outline Map of the Continental United States

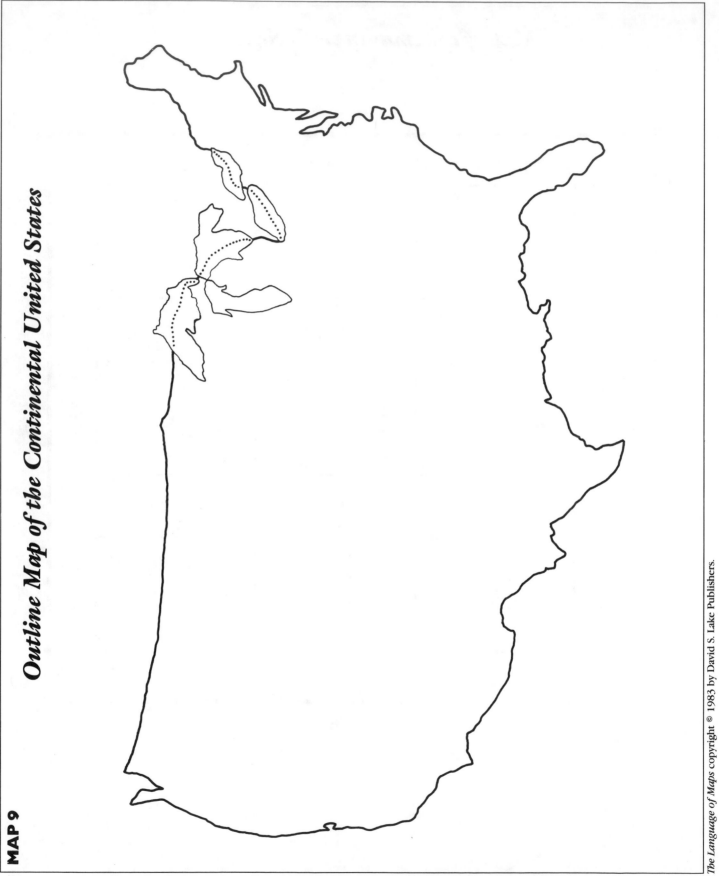

MAP 10

Some Major Canadian Cities

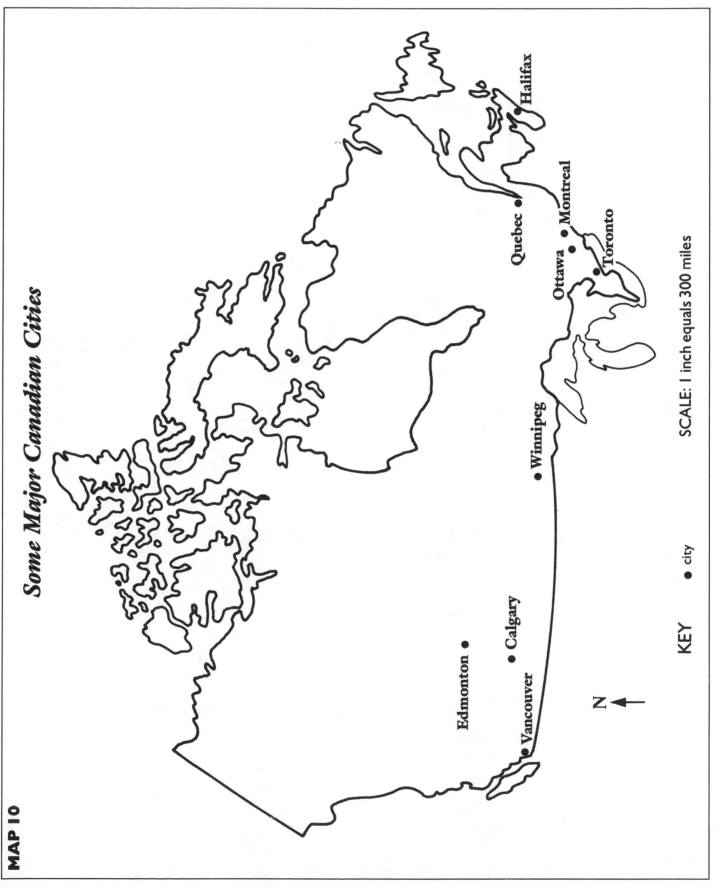

SCALE: 1 inch equals 300 miles

KEY   ● city

N

MAP 11

Part of a Road Map

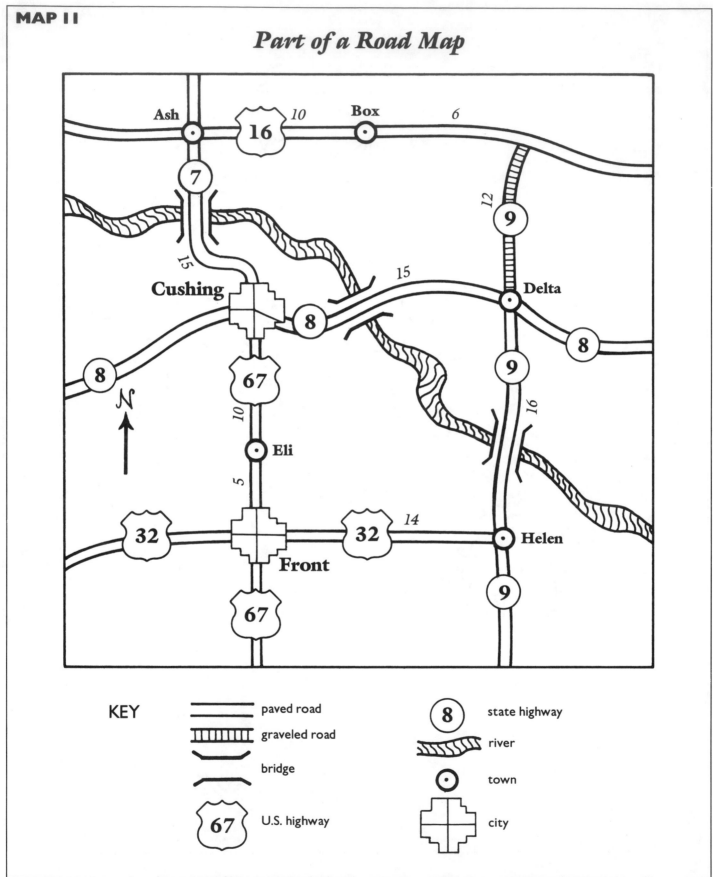

KEY

—————— paved road

||||||||||||| graveled road

⌒⌒ bridge

(67) U.S. highway

(8) state highway

≋≋ river

⊙ town

city

MAP 12

Physical Map of North America

North Pole

ARCTIC OCEAN

GREENLAND

Bering Sea

Beaufort Sea

Baffin Bay

Yukon River

Mackenzie River

Arctic Circle

Labrador Sea

Peace River

Hudson Bay

St. Lawrence River

PACIFIC OCEAN

Columbia River

Great Lakes

ATLANTIC OCEAN

Great Salt Lake

Missouri River

River

Ohio River

Colorado River

Arkansas River

Mississippi

Red River

Rio Grande

Gulf of Mexico

Tropic of Cancer

Gulf of California

Caribbean Sea

SOUTH AMERICA

Panama Canal

KEY

0   400   800

miles

mountains

plains or lowlands

rivers

MAP 13

Selected Cities of North America

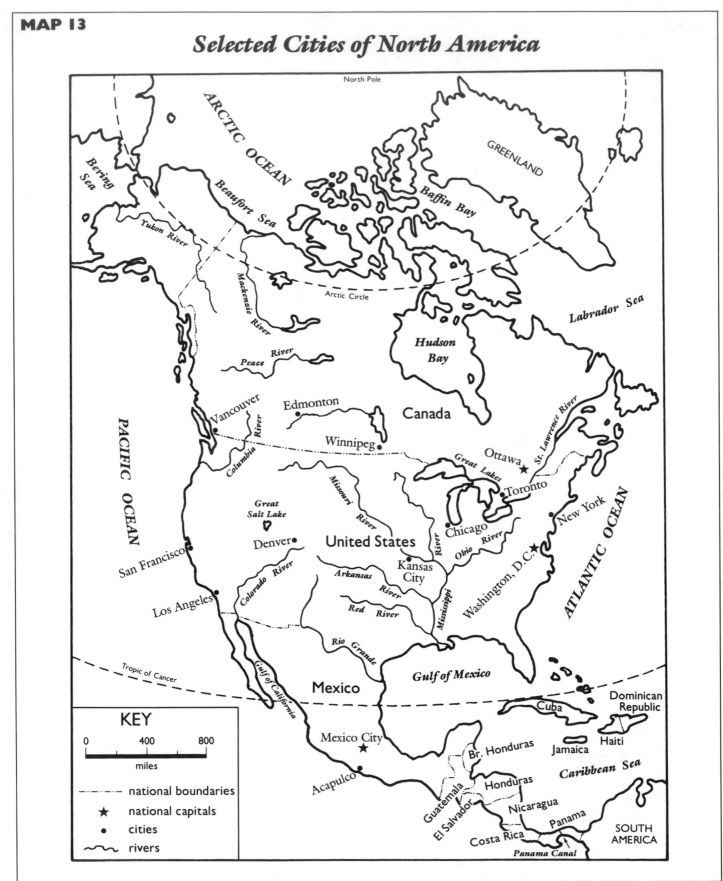

MAP 14

Cities and Rivers of the Western United States

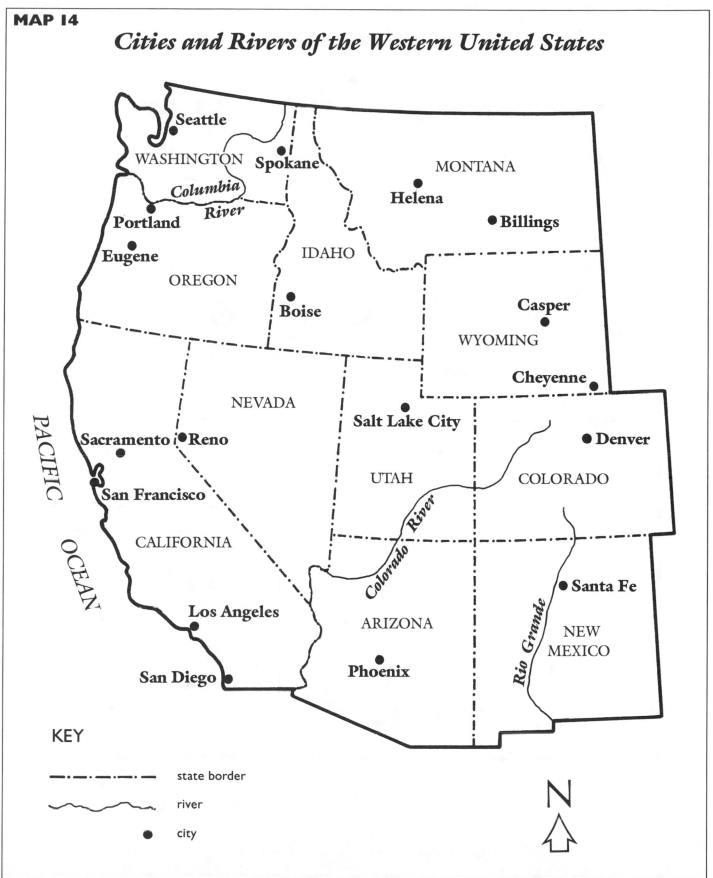

KEY

—··—··— state border

~~~~~ river

● city

N

MAP 15

Part of a Town

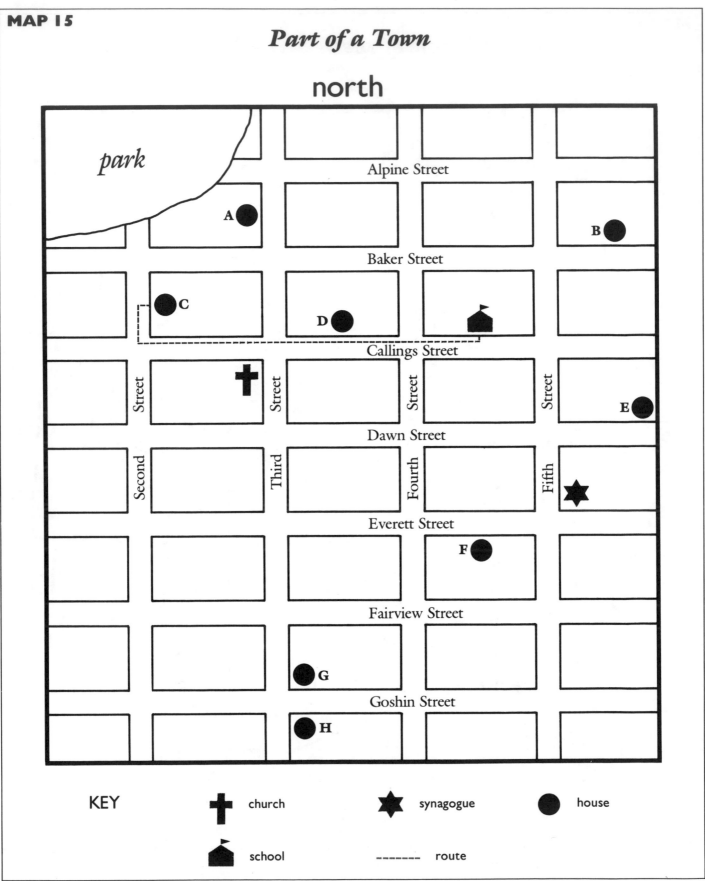

The Language of Maps copyright © 1983 by David S. Lake Publishers.

MAP 16

Road Map of Part of the Great Lakes Area

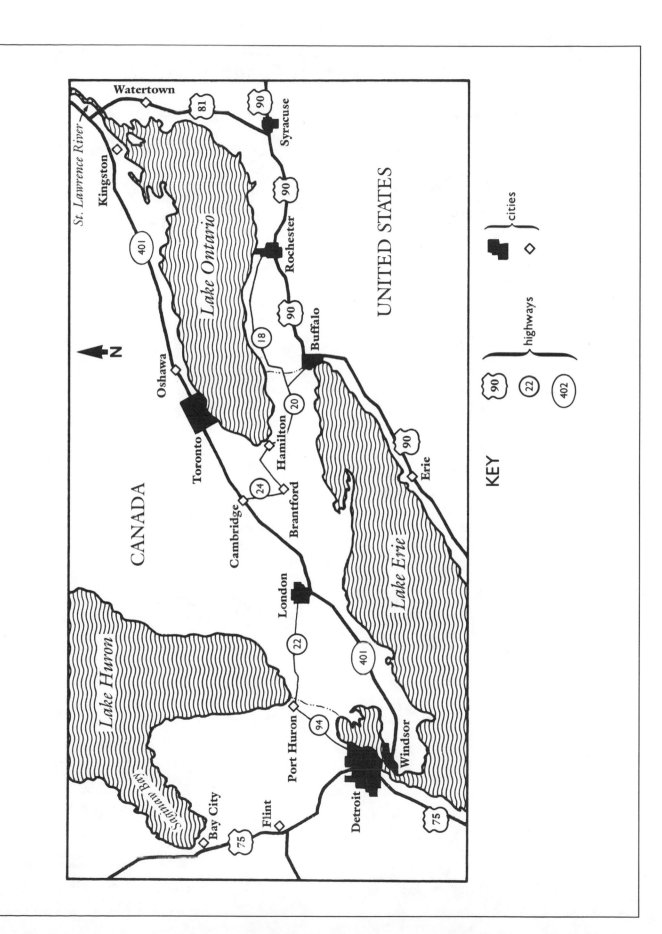

MAP 17

Selected Cities of South America

Barranquilla

Caracas

Georgetown   Paramaribo

Bogota   Cayenne

Cali

Quito   Sao Luis

Guayaquil   Belem

Cerro de Pasco   Recife

Lima   Salvador

Cuzco   Brasilia

Arequipa   La Paz

Iquique   Sucre

Sao Paulo   Rio de Janeiro

Asuncion   Santos

Tucuman

Valparaiso   Rosario

Santiago   Buenos Aires   Montevideo

Concepcion   La Plata

Bahia Blanca

KEY

● city

✪ capital city

SCALE

0	miles	1000

0	kilometers	1600

About the Author

Haig A. Rushdoony is presently Professor of Education at California State College in Stanislaus, California. He teaches social studies classes for beginning teachers and graduate courses in reading and content research.

Haig has taught map-reading and social studies skills to primary-through college-level students. He also has conducted workshops and conferences in geography and social studies for teachers of all levels.

His articles on map reading have appeared in more than 20 publications, including *The Social Studies Review, Elementary School Journal,* and the *Journal of Geography.*

When he's not busy teaching, writing, or finding new ways to teach the language of maps, Haig likes to travel, listen to music, and collect stamps that have map motifs.

Haig lives in Dublin, California, with his wife, Vula.